AN ENCYCLOPEDIA OF BENDING TIME

An Encyclopedia of Bending Time by Kristin Keane
Copyright © 2022 by Kristin Keane. All rights reserved.

Published by Barrelhouse Books
Baltimore, MD

www.barrelhousemag.com

Published in the United States of America

ISBN 13: 979-8-9850089-0-6

First Edition

Cover design: Shanna Compton
Page design: Adam Robinson

An ENCYCLOPEDIA
of BENDING TIME

═══ *Kristin Keane* ═══

a memoir

Every empirical law has the disquieting quality
that one does not know its limitations.

—EUGENE WIGNER

CONTENTS

An Encyclopedia of Bending Time
1

Index of Entries
121

Works Referenced
123

Acknowledgements
127

About the Author
129

An ENCYCLOPEDIA of BENDING TIME

ABSOLUTE TIME exists apart from observation. It can only be rendered through math, flowing through the universe at a scale at which externalities such as birth and death go unaccounted for. It is unforgiving. Astronomer and physicist Isaac Newton promoted the concept when he claimed in *Philosophiae Naturalis Principia Mathematica*, "All motions may be accelerated and retarded... but the flowing of absolute time is not liable to any change. The duration or perseverance of the existence of things remains the same, whether the motions are swift or slow, or none at all." In contrast, relative time moves by way of our observation of change: the rotation of the Earth, the cycle of the moon.

I had never thought about time that way much before, but I understand now how the tide and it are the same, how they both ebb. When did we stand together at the sea's edge? I'm not certain. Now, I try to count: my hands, your hands, our feet pressed into sand. Did we smile? Were the shells you collected all whole? How do I answer these questions?

Do you know what the edge of the water is called where it froths and washes everything away that is not stayed down? I can't ask you anymore. It is a border, I know. A kind of fringe. There is so much there in its boundary, parts of animals and the sea pushed against the beach: you and me, now separated.

See also BEING; NEWTON, SIR ISAAC; MEMORIES; RETURNS; TIDES.

AFTERLIFE. Now, I turn to the familiar scripts of lives altered but returned: the VHS tapes we kept in the curio cabinet decades ago I watched as a child. *Beetlejuice* (1988), *Pet Sematary* (1989), *Ghost*

(1990), and *The Crow* (1994) depict varying circumstances of life after death, and all rely on traditional story constructions to frame its possibilities: hauntings, longings, returns. In all four films, central characters become aware death has deprived them of the thing they once were. In the '90s, I watched these with strips of candy buttons and a remote control. They aim to display the gruesome artifacts of life's end and the munificent hosts who carry protagonists through to meaningful understanding. Surely there is something here for me now inside their variance.

Afterlife indicates the open-ended time that begins when life ends. It is a beginning *after* an ending. The afterlife is for the dead, yet its time holds an essential consideration for the living: a kind of hope.

For Sigmund Freud, belief in the afterlife—an idea whose reverberations have found their way into history, philosophy, psychology, theology, and popular culture for centuries—protected the psyche from confronting the meaninglessness of death. In *The Future of an Illusion*, he wrote that believers in the afterlife view death as an extension of existence that is perhaps closer to a sublimity not found on earth. I never asked you if you thought you would find perfection at the end of your breath, but you did believe in a kind of continuation.

I am searching for a guide somewhere in the ephemera of our lives together: our stories were also entangled with the ones we watched. My memory functions like a pinball machine now: a plunger catapulting recollections into bumpers made from artifacts of our time together.

I have the flowers I gave you, once pressed between the pages of a yellowed album. Red roses aged into boysenberry as thin as onion skins—and yet, and *yet*—are they dead if they are still here decades after I pulled them from their roots and pressed them into your hands? I cannot go back to my conception of Beetlejuice's loss of self, the resurrection and return of things so beloved three decades ago. What did *I* know about missing, then? Now I only have *things*—flowers. Slim representations of the loss of a mother.

A blossom becomes alive and then it is not alive. Is it still a blossom?

Where did you go?

See also MOVIES; FREUD, SIGMUND.

AJAR. When your parents upgraded automobiles in the '80s, you inherited their gunmetal Chrysler LeBaron. The rims of the car were shined to a gleaming silver, spoked like bicycle wheels. The pristine interior had a velvet upholstery, fancy buttons pre-tuned to radio stations J and I fought to control. It was nothing like the station wagon you packed us into when you and our father divorced only a few years before—a clunky brown machine, with room enough inside for a large animal.

You loved the LeBaron's gleam. You'd deposit a Stevie Nicks tape into the deck and blast her anthems through the windows with a gripping new kind of independence. I wish I could see your hair swept out the window again: ribbons of gold.

After work, you would retrieve us. Me, from the place I got drunk on daytime soap operas and cartoons, gameshows and syndicated sitcoms, rooted at the television in my grandmother's sunken living room, my fingers dusted with the crumb-ends of Nilla Wafers. Sometimes J waited there, too, or at a neighbor's nearby, making friendship bracelets and painting fingernails, things I didn't yet have interest in. I had too many stories to study. After, I'd emerge from my zombie trance and stagger to the window where I'd wait for your headlights to appear in the dark, characters and story arcs swelling in my mind.

Once at home, you'd slide the car into the driveway and we'd race out—the ends of backpack straps trailing on the ground, my untied shoelaces dripping with puddle water. You'd put your head out the window: "Girls!" you'd shout from the driver's seat to us. *"Girls!"* We'd clamor at the front door while you pointed to the refuse left on the backseat and stuffed into the console: the plastic casing of a Laffy Taffy bar, a pair of Keebler peanut butter crackers smashed at a seatbelt's buckle.

The car. Stevie Nicks. Television episodes. Just us girls. Time was passing and I never once considered it.

The door is ajar, a robotic narrator vocalized from a speaker in the LeBaron's front paneling, reminding us to close everything. That was my favorite part—the idea that someone lived inside who understood when something was undone. Someone who was accounting for things. *Noticing.*

I think about them so often now. About doors and memories and things which are partway open.

You were not sick.
And then they told us you would become sick.
And then you were sick.
And then you were gone.
Disappeared.

ALICE'S ADVENTURES IN WONDERLAND. Produced in 1985, *Alice in Wonderland* is a two-part, star-studded television film based on Lewis Carroll's *Alice's Adventure in Wonderland* (1865) and its counterpart, *Through the Looking-Glass, and What Alice Found There* (1871). You recorded it on VHS tapes J and I memorized word-for-word. Summer afternoons while you worked, we turned up the air conditioning and danced to the songs in our pajamas before riding bicycles to the liquor store to buy candy cigarettes. As in the original work, after tumbling down a rabbit hole, Alice—the protagonist—meets characters through a variety of encounters which motor the narrative plot as she attempts to make her way back home.

In the second part of the television film, Alice remains confined to another universe behind the living room mirror as regular life appears to go on in time without her. Only when she convinces herself the monster she's envisioned exists solely in her imagination is she able to finally make her way home, escaping the Looking-Glass world where she has experienced everything in a kind of upside-downness. In the last scene, her mother awakens her in the living room.

For one hundred eighty-three minutes, Alice is presented with an inverted reality: a caterpillar the size of a man, animals who address her with various dilemmas. She must parse non-sensical turns of phrase.

I am not saying we are the same, Alice and I. But the script of that story—written into my bones as a child like so many others I watched—forms an entry point for making sense of this disorientation, *my* new tumbling. Underneath the color, and each bizarre encounter, is Alice's enduring desperation to understand her experience, and to recover the thing which is missing.

See also HOME.

ALPHABET comes from the first two letters of Greek, *alpha* and *beta*—both derived from Phoenician letters: the former from *aleph*, related to the Semitic word for ox; the latter from *bayt*, or *bet*, meaning "house."

"A" is for "absolute time," "afterlife," "Alice's Adventures in Wonderland." "A" is also for our other artifacts: "Ayrshires," and "Arizona." We had a beginning together and then an ending, and now I have a new beginning you're not a part of, unlike alphabets fixed into a permanent kind of order.

It is important to arrange these words now, to write us into something. I can take events, put them down in a line: you became pregnant in 1980; I was born the next year in the winter. In 1989, *Pet Sematary* provided me with one framework for the afterlife. We lived together until 1999.

Timelines also have many constraints: reviewing each year suggests access to a kind of total recall I don't have. I tell you this now, so we both understand the kaleidoscopic tumbling of memory is only a *kind* of truth that cannot be so tidily arranged. Perhaps a syllabary would center me—maybe in listing, I will find you inside somewhere, materialized back into your regular shape.

I'm trying to say I am attempting to contain myself—to contain you. To find the ridges of each of us and where our borders rest so I can figure out how to traverse them. To organize the things we are made of: magic and television and long stretches of apartment-rental shag carpeting. Your eyes and the shells on the beach.

See also RESIDUE; TOTAL RECALL.

ALTARS you assembled first appeared in the '80s. They collected on your dresser top: lumps of agate set beside a blue jay feather. Next, there were cards—small glossy strips marked with adjectives and nouns like "light," and "peace." You incorporated animal bones, small teeth and claws, photographs and sometimes notes scripted in your perfect handwriting. Over the years, you brought them wherever you went. Whenever you came to stay with me and B you dedicated the end of our coffee table or the credenza to your arrangements—a small leather bag filled with sand set beside our wedding photograph. A pebble dipped in red paint.

Why, in all this time, did I never once ask you to read them to me, to point at each object and explain what story you were telling and to whom? You constructed them in my very own living room with the care of a watchmaker and I never even asked you why. What did each object mean? What did you think about when you touched them with your hands?

See also TAXIDERMY.

ARIZONA is one of fifty American states. Located in the Southwest, it's home to nearly seven-and-a-half million residents. Petrified forests have been raised from the desert and canyons carved into the topography by centuries of tectonic activity and erosion from wind and water. In Sedona, some believe the rock formations produce energy centers that visitors can access for healing.

Arizona, you always said, felt like home.

In the '80s, you saved for months to journey there for a retreat. The women stripped down to nothing; they dunked themselves in mud baths and howled at the moon. They were all grieving something, you said. You, you were trying to figure out—after you'd started your life over, after you'd left a marriage and reclaimed time—who you really were.

Once, when we looked through photographs right before you disappeared, we came to a small stack of images of you barefoot in red soil, your white t-shirt stamped with chalky earth.

"Where were J and I?" I asked.

"Probably with your grandparents then, I don't remember." You paused, looked at the photograph. "That was a long time ago. Like another life."

I wish I could ask you now how you handled all the change that came with starting a new beginning. How you leaned into time's bending.

ARROWS are used in physics to describe the way time functions: a kind of signifier, the reference to time's arrow—the signified. In *The Order of Time*, Carlo Rovelli notes how the unalterable past produces both positive and negative associations, while the future exclusively contains unpredictability. Since the past cannot be reshaped, the future is separated from it not with a line, but an arrow.

I can write us in a line: you became pregnant in 1980; I was born the next year in the winter. In 1985, *Alice's Adventures in Wonderland* and *Through the Looking-Glass* were adapted into a television musical J and I viewed repeatedly. In the '90s I watched the Ronco Electric Food Dehydrator infomercial on daytime television, memorizing the script for a product we could not afford to buy. It was a story like every other: a protagonist who wanted something while a pressure cooker of time boiled underneath her.

I could rearrange the order—that is one way I could organize time with you. More alphas and betas put into stories which are now twisted, upended. After 1999, there were twenty more years. There were more flowers dried into paper-thin knots, little devotions we exchanged with one another. More stories, more suns and moons and celestial reorderings making up days, weeks, months.

Here, I cannot shift the course of these things and I cannot keep the arrow from moving forward. But in Rovelli's work I cling to a simple concept that works as a fingerhold: the future, he says, *can* be shaped. Anything is possible because it does not yet exist.

Meaning: there might be a time again when I find you, a way to take the dots on the past's line and shift them another direction, one we do not yet understand.

See also BASELINE; HAWKING, STEPHEN; POPEIL, RONALD.

AYRSHIRES. Known for their heartiness and resistance to drought, Ayrshire roses can grow in very harsh soil conditions. Typically fragrant, their dark glossy leaves grow from long canes, with purple buds springing to bloom annually in pinks or whites. Easily trained, they follow direction well if provided enough structure. You grew roses in the backyard along the fence.

In the field of semiotics, a signifier (a word, an image) and a signified (what the signifier represents) make a sign. In *Mythologies*, Roland Barthes writes that myths are made when complete signs are used as signifiers to create a message. For example, *Pet Sematary's* scenes depict the dead coming back to life, but as myth they signify a more complex message about the dangers of refusing to let the dead go. Glyphs of arrows can form myths about direction. A photograph of you in the mud, a myth of freedom. Barthes says of roses, that though the rose acts as a signifier to signify passion, the rose can't act as the sign alone. The rose alone is "empty." Together, with the signifier, they are "full." They are a sign.

You loved roses—I pressed them into your hands to mean beauty. Now that you are gone, their message has changed: they are only a *memory* of beauty, now.

Pet Sematary, arrows, a photograph of you, and the roses I pressed into your hands—these are containers, structures I can put us into to understand their shape. They are representations. All of these things had a meaning, and now all those meanings have changed.

Yes—I will need to account for the changes.

Time is the signifier, the signified, and the myth now. It has warped us.

A blossom develops and then it is not alive but is it still a blossom: how can we understand what time does if you are nowhere, but a rose withered from its stem is still visible, dead, but here?

BAKULA, SCOTT (1954-PRESENT) is a television actor best known for his performances as Captain Jonathan Archer on *Star Trek: Enterprise* and as Dr. Sam Beckett on *Quantum Leap*—two of twenty-five roles included in *TV Guide's* "Legends of Sci-Fi." Born in St. Louis, Missouri, Bakula has been nominated for five Primetime Emmy Awards. His mother's name is Sally Bakula, née Zumwinkel.

Both *Quantum Leap* and *Star Trek: Enterprise* concern themselves with notions of time travel: visiting the past and future, mirror universes, the confounding nature of the spacetime continuum. They both also explore ideas of home, mortality, and returns.

I didn't know, when I watched them with you growing up, how I was swallowing these narratives. How I was putting time and all its sorrowful puzzles into me, learning that it motors stories which edifices hold up—first a desire, then a problem, and finally, a resolution.

Lately I've been consumed with the idea of portals, fourth dimensions and tesseracts. I spent the better part of a summer after your diagnosis reviewing *Quantum Leap* reruns. Now, I keep looking. Bakula's Sam Beckett has built the Project Accelerator, a time-leaping device funded by the government. In a desperate act to save the project from termination, he tests the device too early, gets launched through time into an Air Force test pilot's body—you remember the premise, don't you? Tasked with changing history, each episode casts him into a scenario he must somehow repair or prevent: an accident, health crisis, murder, suicide. His is a permanent displacement, a resetting of the course of history. In the first episode, Sam suffers amnesia. Over time, his memory returns bit by bit, but he never gets to return home—they need him to always embody another soul, exist as something different from his real self. "They" is ambiguous. Is it God or fate or time? The patient audience guesses alongside him.

You were sitting *right there* as we watched episode after episode.

I might have looked over at you, and you might have smiled.

See also CABO SAN LUCAS; NOVIKOV SELF-
  CONSISTENCY PRINCIPLE.

BARTHES, ROLAND (1915-1980). A French philosopher and semiotician, Barthes is the author of *Mythologies*, an exploration of the meaning of art, literature, food, and how popular culture creates myths from such things. Barthes was concerned with signs, interpretations, and relationship patterns inside of systems, like how roses carry messages of passion, or how arrows suggest motion or direction.

The day after his mother died in 1977, Barthes began writing reflections of her death on small strips of paper. The collection of three-hundred thirty cards was published first in France as *Journal de deuil*, and later translated as *Mourning Diary*. "I know now that my mourning will be *chaotic*," he wrote just a week after her passing, later stating that he wanted to stay home in order to tend to flowers he set at her bedside, so he could keep them from wilting.

Barthes recorded reflections for two years—from the fall of 1977 to the summer of 1979—while he wrote other works. Note by note, he attempted to record and make sense of his mother's passing in a collection of reflections accumulated into a postulation of a book. In October, one of his earliest entries concerns the effect of the death-event. He notes how after someone dies, the future itself becomes a sort of unhinged manufacturing of time he refers to as "futuromania."

See also CHANGE.

BASELINE typically refers to the starting point of a variable before a condition is applied, used later to measure the magnitude of its effect. One's baseline could comprise one's relationships to various aspects of life before a major life-changing event occurs: how much time one spends working, how much personal privacy one requires, whether or not one believes in God, or whether one thinks at all about the sea or the tide or time.

You took pleasure in the idea of the afterlife and I did not; you worshipped what could not be seen, and I did not.

Once, you asked me why. I had searched, but could not pull a kind of God from the folds.

Now, wherever it is you've gone—unobservable to me—is all I think about. What even *is* time there?

See also BLUR; SEA.

BEGINNING. *In the beginning* is the first phrase in the book of Genesis; *let's begin* initiates action during a gathering; *begin again* signals a re-attempt when things have taken a bad turn. These are just signals.

We have to find a way to start.

I will confess I am hoping for a way to put this in order so I can bend time to my will. A typology holds a certain appeal; I am good with structure, after all. Remember how well I always followed the rules? How lost I became if they went blurry? My brain works best in systems, in forms, the fixed order of the alphabet a firm boundary with shape: each of our items with its set of facts.

Mathematical models are often comprised of equations with a variable representing time. Perhaps I can do the same with our objects: take your crystals and our television shows, and angle things that have already happened to shape a story which has gone off the rails without you here. Maybe the objects can stand in for these abstract letters and strings of numbers I do not understand. You could be the x in the equations, and I could be the y—being away from you as a child gave me stomachaches.

What if I tried harder to find meaning in this rearrangement of artifacts? I have come to the cruel conclusion, quite immediately, that they are what I am left alone with. The alphabet split apart like a pomegranate; the seeds—each one—a memory or imagining, small as letters, broken open. Maybe there will be clues inside of them for how exactly to find you.

Yes, this is about putting boundaries around the things we are made of: roses and Arizona and too much television. Lists can go unfinished, they can continue for always. I like the idea of going on with you this way, writing you into something to keep you here, to keep the tide from washing you away. It is a control, a system I can understand. It is a way to reshape the concept of a beginning to my own liking.

See also ALPHABET.

BEING. It occurs to me in slicing our life into bits with a time-knife and examining us and time in another way, I might find parts worthy of further investigation. My memories hang on either assured details, or float in a murky pool of *maybe.* They seem, even, to shift. Take, for instance, the case of Scott Bakula. Bakula is *Quantum Leap.* Bakula is us on the couch and a leisure activity we shared when you came home exhausted from work. But expanding that memory and others like it could help me make sense of how strangled I feel when I see a photograph of you—put words to the feeling inside my throat where all my sadness appears to migrate. Being varies—there is Before Me and Before You, and After You and After Me. Sam and the Project Accelerator.

Reactions to *Quantum Leap*

Remember how I covered my eyes through the opening credits because the whizzing timeline and the way Sam Beckett dissolved into light beams always frightened me? If material constitution is not an identity, then what is? What about subcutaneous melanoma? What about how you slowly got sicker?

Quantum Leap's conceit violates a number of theories of time travel, including the "shoot the grandfather" paradox, which states that travelling back in time and killing one's own progenitor before they're able to bear children would erase the possibility of the time traveler's *own* material existence. They would risk disturbing the entire historical text of every event that follows the one they've disarranged.

A Photograph of You

I can hardly bear to look at my favorite picture of you. A slim blonde in a bathing suit, younger than I am now, standing on a beach in a frothy ridge of tide. A before-time. A before-daughters. You're slight as ever, hair blown into tendrils by the sea breeze, laughing heartily with your eyes fixed on the water, a savage ocean at your feet. I'd guess there were octopuses nearby then, watching you, curling their arms like ribbons on the cap of a breaker, just outside the frame. You are stunning in that photograph, but that is not why I can't look.

Time: you in it before I was being. Before the arrow advanced and you and I were being together.

That is why I can't look.

The Initial Confounding Moments

In *Quantum Leap*'s first episode, Sam wakes up in a bed not his own, inside the body of a man named Tom Stratton. He asks himself where he is. He asks himself *who* he is.

Facing the Adversarial Effects of Disease

I begin to think about disrupting our entanglements by examining the vocabulary for the rashes on your skin and the small pills you took; every bit of news had been worse than the last. A single sentence uttered by your oncologist, a visual image of your lungs— *Look here, when I zoom in. See that? See how much it has grown?* —our time together reduced down to smudges of letters, syllables, mathematical pathology equations neither of us understood. I was reminded, much more often than I liked, how such small things carry hefty weight: the petal of a rose, an arrow's sharp end. The way the x crosses itself.

Sorrow

Soon, when Sam begins recalling details of his own life, an opportunity emerges to take advantage of his circumstance: his father died in 1976, yet he finds himself in the year 1956. Invigorated by the chance to speak with him again from the past, he sits at the telephone and stares longingly at the dial's numbers, hope immediately deflated: he can't even remember his own last name.

Acts Before Bad News

Once, the morning before a procedure, I took you to walk on that same beach you stand on in my favorite photograph of you. You collected broken sand dollars and put your hands toward the sky as if proselytizing. I took a picture of you at the creamy edge of the tide because I knew someday I would want to remember you that way, arms up like a cross, even though right then, it was very hard to look. There was so much fear in the sand, so much fear in what being even meant to me.

In a thought experiment about the ship of Theseus, the thinker Plutarch asked if, as a famous ship's parts were replaced one by one over time, it would become an entirely different ship than the ship it once was. There were no ships on the horizon that day, but I thought of that paradox anyway because I seemed to understand already that it was best to ready myself for a kind of disappearing. That is: you, gone.

Sam must embody others to put things right—reunite family members, change the outcome of a basketball game, protect someone's life. Sam, I think, can teach me something if I go back and examine him more carefully. He and I have more in common than we used to—like him, I am now sideways, heart-sick, not myself. I am the character who has been inverted, deposited into another dimension where time does not feel like an arrow, but like a compass-needle pointed everywhere. The things I know are now upside down, reversed.

How did Sam treat that—the disarray? I try to remember.

In a season two episode, he takes on the life of a single mother living in Arizona whose teenage son is kidnapped. I watch for clues. I evaluate the portrayal of a woman facing the edges of loss and peril, desperate for a life raft. Maybe I could learn something about confronting fear, about endurance, about manifesting time more flexibly. What did you think when we watched that episode together in the '90s? Before, I only saw the children in the episode. Now all I can see is *you*.

The miracle is a man in a time machine changing the course of an entire family's future.

All we wanted was a miracle made from letters, syllables arranged in a different order, with different words that didn't wrestle up so much worry about the future. We wanted antidotes to "terminal" and "aggressive" to change our perception of the forthcoming time.

You are not here, but I still want that. I want to understand it.

Questions
Yes. This is one way of finding you, of lining up the parts of a part. I can take events, endeavor to see more deeply inside them: us on the couch with *Quantum Leap* and you at the beach. Then bad news. Then questions about how to form this into a story, such as: In narratives foreshadowing her inevitable death, when does the mother usually die? What happens to protagonists *when* the mother dies? How does one find their mother again, given the limitations of the third dimension? What role does time play in altering one's relationship to the mother in the past, present and future—meaning, after *she*, the mother, is no longer being?

See also OCTOPUSES; PLUTARCH.

BETWEEN TIME is the middle of two events, a space for waiting. It is the same as the "meantime," "meanwhile," "interim." *Between jobs, between relationships, between appointments.*

Experiments have demonstrated that people estimate enjoyable events as taking less time than unenjoyable ones. Some researchers believe successful memories are better organized and occupy less cortical space, therefore are only *experienced* as taking up less time. Alternatively, the greater the urgency and pain of an experience, the more slowly time appears to pass in retrospective memory.

Early in the summer, just months before you disappeared, I lost partial hearing in my right ear. During minor episodes of vertigo in the first days of June, it sounded as if a sea churned inside my head. An ear irrigation had no effect and the sea only crashed with more force; traversing the hallway in the morning felt as if I was walking across the deck of a ship turned on its side.

At the hearing clinic, I sat in a darkened booth. A woman handed me a set of headphones and spoke to me through a tiny microphone located in another room. There were small chairs, diagrams with colorful images of various procedures pinned to the wall: *This is how you push the buttons. This is how you ask for help with your hands.* She asked me to say *kite, sub, pike, wind.* A series of beeps commenced which I held my hand up to signal I heard. She asked me to click when the recording said *ice cream, hot dog, sunset, sundae.* In the space between the sounds I wondered what I *wasn't* hearing, if in fact I was missing the signals she had shot across the line. I clicked. I deliberated whether or not I was imagining beeps between the words which all seemed to evoke the nonchalance of summer—a very foreign feeling then, even though it was June. Afterwards, she came out of the booth.

"Your hearing is fine," she told me, jotting a note on her clipboard. As she said this, I heard the swooshing, the seashells gently clanging in my ears.

"What about the nausea?" I said. "What about all the infections I've had?"

She looked up.

"I'm supposed to go on a trip next week. How will I swim in the sea?" I didn't mention the urgency I felt about swimming with you there. How suddenly you were tired all the time. How we had collected so much bad news in all the waiting, between things. Two months earlier, doctors had asked us to carefully examine a black-and-white image of your lung tissue, to notice how the spots changed shape in the collagen fibers since your last scan. Since then, a swell was building.

She put her hands at her waist and tapped her foot.

"Do you want to see a specialist, then?" she asked, as if it was an accusation. She was done with me.

In the parking lot, I could hear the ocean, the boat in my ear about to capsize. I went home and lay down again to make the spinning stop, wondering if the sea was like the beeps—a thing just out of reach.

I can get through this, I thought. Then: *I can't get through this. See also* DIAGNOSIS.

BLAINE, DAVID (1973-PRESENT). A magician, Blaine places himself in coffins and ice blocks, feasts on glass, brings animals back from the dead. In "Dressed for Dinner"—a stunt video shot to promote a line of men's suits—he swims with great white sharks off Guadaloupe's coast. He wants the viewer to understand this could go on forever. He could smoke cigars, eat bananas underwater, time would go on, and he'd remain unafraid of what's to come.

Or would he? The knife's edge of death turns slowly in circles below where he suspends in the water. Some of us can endure better than others, he seems to be saying. He seems to be interrogating something about time, about getting through an impossibility—or at least his relationship to it. That to put oneself in obvious peril communicates one has let go of what it means to care about endings, about time *stopping*.

An illusion is a misperception, which makes something appear to be something else. Typical examples include card tricks, ventriloquism, pulling a rabbit from a hat. In these cases, an illusion*ist*—someone performing—takes responsibility for the false impression, an act of entertainment. People can also create illusions for themselves, tricking their minds into beliefs in order to protect themselves from inevitable truths, to whisper inside their own ears that everything will be okay, that everything will be *fine*.

I believed there was a way to shiver out of a loss that was already planted inside the horizon line—that I could *evade* it somehow, slough it off.

Denial can be a type of illusion, too—a refusal of the thing which can be seen, obfuscating a truth that cannot be accepted. People deny obsessions, addictions, and sometimes their own mortality—even a loved one's death.

One afternoon, I watched as Blaine broke a world record for oxygen-assisted static apnea on the *Oprah Winfrey Show*, holding his breath underwater for seventeen minutes. I fell in love with theatrical proxemics that afternoon. I fell in love with the idea that the space between two things conveys its own signal, its own kind of sign. I had studied television for years, learning about story structure, lessons, themes—but here was a man playing with the *viewer*. It was a different kind of script, a sort of law-bend. It was as if he was communicating to the audience that rules were only inventions, and with the right kind of will, one could make anything go their way.

He floated in a sphere of water and that suspension was a message, a reach.

Blaine's mother died of cancer thirteen years before.

See also MAGIC; X; Y.

BLUR. "Blur" is a variant of "blear," which some definitions describe as a blinding or dimming of vision through tears, or of figuratively hoodwinking. Meaning: it is a thing that is real and also a thing that is not. *To* blur is to make a confusion. *A* blur cannot be seen clearly. Take, for example, raindrops accumulating on a windshield: each droplet creates its own blur, distorting anything appearing beyond it. They cause the driver to initiate the wipers, to clear the windows because the driver's vision has become *blurred*. The objective of the wipers is to *unblur* them.

Blurring can happen unintentionally in optical fields, or in photographs of quickly moving objects. Bokehs are effects which can produce a range of both in-focus and out-of-focus background blurs. Other optical features of images include box blurs, channel blurs, vector blurs and Gaussian blurs, which can all be employed intentionally to enhance certain aspects, or soften the overall appearance of graphic images. "Bokeh" comes from "boke," meaning "fuzziness," like the kind of confusion made from ears filled with the sea.

Time smears my memories like fingers in dabs of wet paint. Sometimes I am not so certain anymore about the accuracy of my recall. A mimesis—is that what this is? How do you stop a memory from becoming fictionalized, or preserve something not written down? How can I review you and me in the same way on the couch with our stories in the '90s, knowing how my memory changes every moment—knowing I have lost so much? Maybe a manipulation of myself doesn't matter, or perhaps this problem is a separate matter beyond finding you.

Photographs of you are hard to examine. They are all in the past tense. In them, you may or may not smile. You may or may not stand in the sea. It confounds me now when I examine images of the Before You, how I can't help but consider all which has occurred in the times in between. In the image of you at the sea, an octopus might have lingered nearby, or perhaps a creature lurked under the wave break outside the frame, just waiting to swim in with bad news. Maybe that creature is the harbinger, or maybe it is just the memories, blurring my reasoning of these things.

"There you go with your imagination, my Kristin," you would say. "It's just a photograph, a nice memory."

"Is it?" I'd ask, as an octopus swam into view while you smiled, admiring the water lapping your feet. Perhaps I am forcing the connections between things. I am, after all, looking everywhere for a sign.

At the carwash in the '80s, we'd roll the windows of the LeBaron up and watch the way the water droplets collected on the glass before they rolled towards one another. Inside, we sat on the buttery charcoal upholstery with the fingerprint-smudged console and tins of hard candies wedged between the passenger seat and plastic buckles. I probably said something like, *Look how they fold together*, and you probably responded by saying something like, *Isn't that so beautiful?*

You were always noticing grace.

Sometimes the droplets joined and then slipped off into the space where the window ended, but sometimes they grew fatter until the machine did the work of disappearing them. They were there on the glass, and then they were not. The track would lead us into the dark and, at the end, you'd drive us back into daylight.

There are so many problems with time I need to already resolve: to find you, to shape the future, change my perception of it.

See also FOG; UNRAVEL.

BORDER. Acting as both a verb and a noun, *borders* concern the boundaries of things. Their *edges*. Space is central to this concept, though objects can be bordered both literally and figuratively. There is an implication of a center and of transgressing a space.

You and I were once separated by our bodies, but where, exactly, is the line between us now, if the place you're in is unknown? I can press my fingers against the wall and say to myself: *This is a kind of line*. I can point to your photograph sitting inside the altar I made for you on a shelf hanging from that same wall, and say: *This is a kind of you*. But you are not on the other side, and I cannot hold the photograph up to your face anymore to compare the difference.

Immaterial borders exist all around us, the line between locations acknowledged on maps, but not always seen.

Where do you even start anymore?

See also ENCYCLOPEDIAS; SEA.

CABO SAN LUCAS. Located in the Mexican state of Baja California Sur at the end of the peninsula, where the Gulf of California meets the Pacific Ocean, Cabo San Lucas has become a heavily touristed destination for beaches, diving, and parasailing. A corridor of hotels, resorts and timeshares line the coast now joining Cabo San Lucas and San Jose del Cabo into a region referred to as Los Cabos.

In June, when we came from the airport to Paraiso Escondido, the roadway fell off through the fingerprint-stained windows of the shuttle, the Sea of Cortes revealing itself in one long stunning azure line behind tennis courts, cabanas, and pools dotting the resort's landscapes like tiny turquoise jewels.

Across the aisle, you smiled at me. At the airport that morning you looked unsteady, complained about your glasses.

"Something's not right with these damn things," you said.

"They're fine," I said. "*You're* fine."

I insisted we go—you and me and J. I insisted on everything then, a bookend to months of bad news. Time, I realized, was a nebulous thing I was attempting to harness. There, you complained about your glasses with your purple sneakers and a rolling suitcase, the small zipper pouches of Kleenex and safety pins tucked inside, but I knew—*we* knew—soon you wouldn't be able to offer me a pair of aspirin, a dry set of socks. Mexico was a proxy for the After Time—where I knew we'd still exist on a plane together. It was a thing I could wrap my hands around. It was something I could cram us inside of.

Four months earlier in February, I took you and J to Seattle where you stood in a stairway and let snow fall onto your face. From the flight of stairs above, I took a photograph of you smiling to yourself where you had taken your jacket off, turned your head up to the sky, and opened your mouth to the snow.

You started coughing in Seattle, like there was a machine inside your chest.

"Just allergies," you said.

In Mexico, too, you coughed as you tooled around the hotel room unpacking your swimsuit, your straw hat.

"Allergies," you said, every time you cleared your throat, but at night, when you wheezed, I lay awake staring at the rotation of the fan on the ceiling, thinking only about Scott Bakula, about that time machine.

We are on vacation, I reassured myself. *So that means everything will be okay.*

See also FOLDS; GONE.

CAST. Both a verb and noun, the former refers to the action of putting something out in such a way as to throw or send. Usually there is an intentional force behind the action as when shaping a kind of material *into* a cast, or forming a collection of actors for a production of a play, television show, or film.

In the latter examples, the cast generally includes a range of actors playing characters reflecting different attributes and habits written into scripts. *Quantum Leap* had Bakula as Beckett and Dean Stockwell as Al. Deborah Pratt voiced both the narrator and Ziggy—the artificial intelligence assisting Sam though his leaps. The 1985 *Alice in Wonderland* adaptation included a variety of stars: Shelley Winters, Sherman Hemsley, Sammy Davis Jr., Ringo Starr, Sally Struthers, and Carol Channing.

I consider the roles in our cast: if I'm the protagonist in this story, what does that make you? And who exactly stars as the *antagonist*—time?

I also must consider the treatment of all our different versions: Before You. After You. Before Me. After Me. Before Time. After Time. Then Time. I'm not sure if the you before is one thing, and the you after, now, something else. I reach to describe your character's attributes and this is where the line blurs: you *must* be inherently different if you are in another dimension, but do you still admire the curves in seashells, the color of birds' feathers? Do you still rise early and meticulously fold your clothes?

Of course there is the other question lingering always in the background like an understudy, one I deeply fear answering: can you still love me anymore?

See also BEING.

CHANGE materializes as a complete metamorphosis or a slight shift in material being, viewed as a kind of recasting or reforming. One can change a standard breakfast order, change trains, change clothes before going to bed, change one's religion, or change height as their body grows. Forms can become entirely different by chang*ing*—*My, have you changed*, one might say in response to a difference in behavior. A tide changes shape—at one moment the edge may resemble the silhouette of a seahorse; in the next, a wedge of cantaloupe. The word change is ergative—both transitive and intransitive at once. It indicates shifting, but also can shift by its use. Typically, little difference exists in the meaning between these versions, but the former puts the emphasis on the subject and its actions upon the direct object, while the latter makes the direct object the subject.

What happened in Mexico changed you, or: *You changed in Mexico.*

Mexico changed our relationship to time, or: *Our relationship to time changed in Mexico.*

What happened in Mexico changed us, or: *We changed in Mexico.*

See also BORDER; SORROW.

CHANNEL. A length of water or a medium to communicate, channels are passageways and a band of frequencies used for radio and television stations. A channel in Cabo San Lucas runs between the marina and the sea.

Let's return to the moments between meeting you at the airport and lying awake considering the Project Accelerator to see if I can make more sense of them:

In the hotel lobby the concierge fastened plastic bands onto our wrists. They resembled those you'd worn for months at the hospital—each colored bracelet you snipped off into a kitchen drawer could be placed into a timeline of bad news: diagnosis, treatment, results, prognosis. The concierge ratcheted yours down to the last possible groove, a tight strangulation against your wrist, swelled from the cabin pressure in the airplane ride from California. He showed us a sleeve of paper laminated in plastic—the television guide in our room—a timeshare suite loaned to us by B's aunt. Menus for the restaurants came clipped to a map of the property, the locations of the pools stippled onto it like cobalt jellybeans—the cabanas and tennis courts, the cages of birds.

The birds! The iridescence of their slick feathers. Peacocks roamed the grounds freely. You pointed. You shouted with enthusiasm.

"Look!" you said. "*Look.*"

On the second day, we took a sunset cruise in exchange for three hours of timeshare tours of ocean-view rooms with paddle fans; artificial apples and bananas glistened perfectly from ceramic bowls. Later, at the harbor, the boat rocked with the wind, the floors coated stickily in spilled cocktails and orange juice from the previous sail.

I took you out to the deck. The mobula rays sprang from the water; they fluttered their sides as if they had wings.

"Look!" you shouted. "*Look.*"

I watched quietly as you took photographs while the wind blew your hair into your eyes. You turned your attention to me and I turned away. I *walked* away. I could not stand to see you in that moment, pulling your hair from your face the way you used to mine, witnessing just what I would miss: time would warp us, I knew. Your hair in your eyes—your hands *pulling* the hair from your eyes—would mean something very different, very soon. I gripped Then Time by my fingertips, tried to sink my teeth into it, but I was wrong in all my approaches: I know now a tenderness had been required that I sometimes could not summon.

In the After Time there would be no boat. No tendrils of hair or fish or sea.

Back in the room we chose *A Star is Born* from the channel guide and ate small cellophane bags of trail mix.

"Oh my god," you said when Bradley Cooper's character hung himself in the garage, his dog whimpering outside the door. You put your hand to your mouth. "He's dead," you said. "I can't believe it."

The next day, you could not get out of bed.

See also ENDINGS.

CHILDHOOD. I studied time travel with you. There was *Quantum Leap*, but also *Early Edition, Babylon 5, Star Trek: The Next Generation, Highlander*—others. Home at night after working, tired and raising two daughters on your own, you'd make silver-dollar pancakes and we'd descend into science fiction, our fingers sticky with syrup.

We often spent Saturdays at the same kind of matinees—stories of cosmic unrest and unrequited love, near-misses of death. To save money, we'd pick our favorite refreshments from the drugstore adjacent to the theater complex: Rolo or Junior Mints for you, Red Vines or Big Hunk for me, a Mounds for J. You'd slide them between the folds in your purse, weighing them down with soda cans obfuscated by your wallet so the ushers who took the tickets wouldn't see them when you opened your bag.

Then, I figured aliens and contemplations of the future just appealed to you. You had an interest in mysticism. Collections of poultices filled with animal bones lined on your dresser alongside tarot cards and wedges of amethyst. You clipped articles about earthquakes from the newspaper and pasted them into notebooks, tracking the barometric pressures with the emergence of migraines. When bad dreams came to me, you'd stand at my bed with your eyes closed, and envision circles of white light around my body to ward off nightmares.

Now, though, I see things differently: you and I were both enraptured by stories of control. Stories where circumstances could be fixed onto the devices of the characters. Stories where people defied odds, righted wrongs, got what they desired in time for the episode's conclusion—or at least tried—as was the case with *Quantum Leap*'s Sam. We wanted alternate universes, miracles, even back then. These stories' premises often defied realities of the ways in which time works.

Then, I immersed myself in sitcoms, daytime dramas. I reconfigured Lego sets into my desires: the primary-colored airport model broke down into the living room of *Family Ties*; the taxicab kit reconstructed into the Hogan family kitchen. You wouldn't watch these with me, though—you wanted only the blurry line between the strange and the real; the almost out of reach. A play with time.

Neither of us cared about time's arrow then; about the way it worked. You relied on the mysterious and magical, things which could not always be seen—and I did not. I wanted form, structure, a reliable formula to help me predict what was to come. That was the difference between you and me. But what now?

In episode three, Sam abandons his mission and instead attends to a timeline in his own life—a violation of Project Quantum Leap's rules. This happens early on, when he's still learning the principles of leaping, and continuing to fill in the spotted "Swiss cheese" of his amnesia. At first, Al refuses to help Sam right events leading to his marriage many years in the future, but eventually he caves, providing Sam with the vital information he needs.

Desire, problem, resolution.

See also ALTARS; TAROT.

CHRONOLOGY. In Berkeley in the '80s, while you cleaned your grandmother's house, I put seed into the edge around the birdbath. At its center was a sundial. I would stand beneath the hydrangea and watch you through the windows: shaking out the rugs, wiping down the counter rimming the drop-in sink. Sometimes you'd see me, and smile through the glass. The shadow at the sundial kept moving, while I tracked its shifting shape.

Let us say that this was my first realization of the concept of time. That this was the part of the story when I noticed, but did not yet understand, how it moved in one direction. At the window through the glass, you were there and so was I.

It could have been this story's prologue.

See also LEIBNIZ, GOTTFRIED WILHELM.

CRYSTALS are three-dimensional collections of atoms or molecules whose repeating patterns construct a lattice. These were objects located on your altars, nestled inside your plants, along your windowsill.

When your grandmother died, you snipped stems of hydrangea from her backyard and set them into a ring of sage and amethyst and animal bone. At her memorial was a table lined with her things—teacups and saucers, mostly, stamped with flowers; small ceramic statues and salt and pepper shakers. Everyone was invited to take something home. Afterwards, in your bedroom, you put a photograph of her beside the altar you constructed, as if to say, *This is the way we say goodbye.*

Or maybe you were saying: *This is the way we keep her here.*

Or maybe you were saying: *This is how we hold on now.*

Or maybe you just gripped something by your fingernails because you did not understand the difference between the Before Time at her kitchen window, washing her dishes while she sat in the living room with a cup of tea, and the After Time when she became not here, the bird bath dried up, seeds scattered on the grass below while the shadow of the sundial kept moving.

See also KNOT; RECOGNIZE.

DEATH. The concept of death for humans is typically developmental. Understanding progresses from a lack of acknowledgment in infancy, to confusion surrounding death's permanence in toddlerhood and young childhood, until finally, understanding its inevitabilities— that all living organisms die because of breakdowns in bodily functions. Images of death portrayed in media such as cartoons and television programs, as well as familial experiences, have influence on when these concepts take root.

While characters often die in stories, on a few occasions, actors have perished during various stages of production, such as Marilyn Monroe, Martha Mansfield, Redd Foxx, James Dean, Bruce Lee, and his son, Brandon Lee. In a number of television shows including *The Young and the Restless*, *Gimme a Break!*, and *Night Court*, the characters of actors who died were recast, killed off the show, or disappeared from the plotline without explanation.

One month after returning from Mexico, you lay in your parents' living room breathing. Just outside the window there was the persimmon orchard and owl house B and I stood underneath to be married. You pointed out the windows. We held your hands. Then something arrived on the horizon I could not see. You looked at it, pointed. Was it time? A kind of light?

J brought objects up from your apartment just adjacent to the persimmon orchard: some of your crystals, a vial of sand, tarot cards. B and I bought a coverlet at the store. *Any requests?* I asked before we went for supplies. You asked for rainbows, mermaids. They had both. We hung colored flags across the window and we played your favorite music. We sat with you on the medical bed that folded in the middle like the flap of an envelope. Our hands all looked the same: mine, yours, J's.

"We love you," we said. Words strangled in my throat. It was the thing always waiting quietly there in the Between Time: the octopus-like form stretching its tentacles into my mouth. I didn't want you to know how scared I was of not understanding who I'd be without you.

She is dying, I had to keep telling myself. *She won't be here in a few days.*

"It's okay to let go," we said. They told us to tell you that at the end. Before you took your last breath, you turned your head to look right at us and a single tear slipped from your right eye and willowed down your face. It happened just like that.

Then you were gone.

You were here, then you were not.

I lay awake that night in the living room where you had been—where J and I slept, the summer moths fluttering at the screen like gray apparitions—awake but already not the same. I tried convincing myself, lying there in the dark with the moths at the window, that you were there. I could conjure the sound of your voice, your eyes—but you were gone. You were disappeared.

What I did not consider then, was the way the moths—whose silhouettes I could see in the moonlight—were beating themselves against the screen. They did not see the border between the place where they flapped and the place they were trying to go. *They* were unaware of this story's inciting event. *They* were unaware you were gone and I had been suddenly launched into the tumbling.

See also AFTERLIFE; INSOMNIA; INSPECT.

DEVOTION comes from the Latin "devovere" meaning to vow, to give of oneself, to promise solemnly. Devotion is an act of dedication, often used to describe one's spiritual worship of God. In religion, devotion relates to the act of prayer or meditation, but also represents an offering of loyalty and fidelity; in secular use, it applies to one's commitment to a person or cause. One can devote themselves *to* something, enact devotion, or *do* devotions.

In Chimayo, a small pilgrimage town in New Mexico directly north of Santa Fe, a small Roman Catholic church made from adobe as red as chestnuts—El Santuario de Chimayo—is believed to help cure cancer, infertility, various diseases of the body.

Late one night in 1810, a religious man stood on the soil of the Los Penientes confraternity, a small patch of land near Chimayo, watching a strange light throb on the hillside adjacent to the Santa Cruz River. He wondered if the pulsing was the effulgence of a riverbank fire. Drawn to the rhythm, he followed it to a place in the ground where a wooden crucifix gleamed with the lambency of a firefly. He took it with him, but the cross had its own spirit, its own portals for relocation: it vanished, and he found it later, alight, on the same patch of earth. It was taken, untethered, and returned three times until with the help of his followers, the man— Bernardo Abeyata—built a chapel around the small hole in the dirt it emerged from. The current-day edifice is erected around it, the pocito of dirt located in a room just beside the church's altar.

The testimonials say rubbing this dirt into the corpus changes one's spirit. They say the dirt and not the crucifix makes the magic, regenerated by the Earth day after day, year after year. Time in this way is unyieldingly generous. It is as if it doesn't matter there.

When I first read about Chimayo, I tried memorizing one particular routine devout pilgrims use, which I found on the website. First, invoke silence; think beyond oneself. Acknowledge all that plagues the body, the heart. Tell God he is needed. Tell him a specific wish, but also relinquish control to his final plan. Finally, rub the dirt on the part of the body in need of healing while summoning Jesus. Finish with a prayer. Say *amen.*

I played the ritual back to myself over and over like a television rerun. I studied its contours, committed it to memory, pictured its sediment drifting through my parts like an hourglass of sand, embedding itself into the neurons, synapses, and cells of each moist organ preparing me to handle the problems of time.

I went there before the end, when it was clear that time with you had already begun to wane. You weren't gone yet, but I wanted to believe there was some kind of preparation for it, a way to seal our borders. It seems important for you to know this now—how hard I was trying to engineer time, how hard I tried. Let's look closer:

A Portal

Testimonials on the church website avow healing, visions of saints and Jesus, sudden recovery from life-threatening conditions—stories of holy earth placed on the knee of a man plagued with leg sarcoma; the hip of a child requiring replacement surgery; the fingers of a mother desperate for her daughter's return from estrangement. The assurance is uncomplicated: put the dirt onto your body and get healed. In one story, a man describes walking beyond the adobe walls of the chapel as descending into a portal.

Portals sounded right. Portals sounded exactly like what I needed: a stir of sacred earth, a bend towards a well of magic, a contact before being set free.

A Manipulation

When I visited Chimayo in the winter before you disappeared, I didn't bring a note, or a gift, just a wish to bend an outcome. I purchased a small tin fixed with an image of the chapel from the welcome center for one dollar. Inside, parishioners gathered, dabbed their foreheads with holy water at the nave. I went to the small chamber room and there was the tiny pocito I read about, no wider than a large bathroom stall. Twelve inches in diameter, the pit resembled a child's sandbox and had two shovels—one black, one orange—sunk into its ground. Alone, I knelt down and dumped a tablespoon of dirt inside the container before screwing it shut.

But the ground did not tremble beneath me. No spontaneous revelations arrived in the adjacent room filled with the discarded aides, photographs, and letters of the devoted who came before me. A placard was nailed to the wall:

If you are blind, weary, suffering from a broken heart, take the high road over the hill. Find the trail that leads you to Chimayo.

Why had I gone there?

Because I had admitted to myself already that the things I thought I believed might not get me through.

A Series of Attempts

Outside in the courtyard, B studied a band of pigeons warming themselves inside a rooftop vent. He smiled, asked if I got what I came for. I nodded quietly, fingering the half-dollar-sized can in my jacket pocket. He took me to the *Welcome to the Prayer Portal* sign where, partitioned into small spaces by wooden posts, four rectangular plywood exhibits stood, protected by guardrails. They were covered in photographs—some just faces, but mostly bodies, too, posed at monuments, sports games, baptisms. Rectangles of people others had loved and come there to get closer to, their photographs offerings, a kind of plea. Babies, grandparents, cousins and daughters each with different arches to their brows, dimples in their chins. Most of them looked very happy. Many by then had probably passed from this dimension, but they were all there looking back at me, a volume of love contained in a very small space.

They were in it together, looking at me from another side, and I was the only one looking back, thinking of you.

Observers aren't allowed to touch the photographs, but I got as close as I could. I took the lid off the can, pinched my fingers into a dab of dirt and put it in my mouth. It was nutty. *Silty*. I leaned in and noticed a very small, unoccupied patch of wall, so I worked it with my imagination like I've always done:

I pictured you in that photograph at the sea—the one before I was born. In the water that day were animals changing themselves when they lost control, dying and being born again, separating from parts of themselves in order to keep going on.

That day in Chimayo, I didn't pray, because I'm not sure how, but I closed my eyes and put myself inside that image. I floated myself above the sea, above the crashing, inside a portal alit with a white line of light. You weren't gone yet, and I meant for the exercise to be a kind of pre-recovery before the fracture—I knew I needed to kill my fear for a particular kind of salvation I would need once you were. Was this the problem, though, or the desire? In typical story arcs they're distinct, although both typically support the self-realization of the protagonist.

Then, I needed a David Blaine-level illusion. I needed to bend time to be with you more: the diagnosis, Seattle, carwashes and nights with you exhausted after pancakes. What was my love? It could be selfish, strangling. I needed things my way. I needed some kind of intervention like the Project Accelerator to transport me to a place where I could be assured that, no matter what happened, I could be with you again.

I needed a time machine.

Now, I need to *understand* time. Maybe that is also a bending—or maybe an illusion will still be required.

You would probably say, "That kind of thinking sounds hard, Kristin." You would probably say, "Some things just can't be explained."

For thirty-one episodes, Sam hopes each leap will send him back from where he came. In episode thirty-two he arrives in a cornfield, dry husks scattered on the ground, their tails rattling in an autumnal breeze. He recognizes the presence of pheasants by their smell, by the desiccated corn husks. Soon he learns he's returned to his childhood home—there is his mother on the porch, his little sister, a brother who will soon be killed—but his mission is not his own. He can't protect his father from dying prematurely, or keep his brother from going to war. He can't save the people he loves. He's there to order a sequence of events—not to fix time for *himself.*

Al acknowledges his suffering, but Sam screams at the cornfields; he shouts into the sky.

He quits.

See also GOBLETS; BLAINE, DAVID.

DIAGNOSIS. Mucosal melanoma, a rare cancer accounting for one percent of melanomas, occurs within mucous membranes lining the body's cavities and is caused by abnormal growth in pigmentation cells in the neck, nose, respiratory tract, eyes, mouth, head, gastrointestinal tract, and other areas. Weak evidence has been found of risk factors including smoking, certain viruses, carcinogens, ill-fitting dentures and, potentially, genetics. Commonly undetected, mucosal melanoma is often aggressive from its first appearance, with cases frequently staging as advanced once identified. Standard treatment options include chemotherapy, immunotherapy, radiation, surgery. Alternative treatment options include tinctures, oxygen chambers, rituals, crystals, green smoothies, marijuana, healing vortexes.

After Mexico, cancer in your brain had spread so much that the radiologist could not account for all the lesions.

"It looks like a constellation of stars," I said when they projected the images. You liked the cosmic imagery but all I could do was think of your glasses, how you had complained about your vision at the airport.

They urged radiation. When your oncologist arrived, she disabused us of other approaches: you would lose speech, she said, and the ability to function. *Things might get really weird for us,* they said.

"How much time?"

"Maybe days," the physicians said. "Maybe weeks. Maybe months—*not* years. We don't like to talk about time," they said.

They always said that.

And yet, and yet, and *yet*—the flowers are no longer living but they are pressed between the pages of an album even though they died before you were sick, even though they died before a time in Mexico when you swept your hair from your face and then later that day said, very softly, *I need to lie down.*

The flowers are still here, shriveled, purple as fruit.

When you called me on the telephone two years before you disappeared, you swallowed and said, "They found something." That could have meant anything—keys, a lottery scratcher, the old Beatles ticket stub you once kept tucked inside a Bible.

I looked at my legs. I wore running shorts. A pair of shoes with a dried strip of mud across the toe. You breathed on the other end of the line and I felt a trapdoor fall open inside myself. *That's* when time became a problem.

Running shorts. Tennis shoes. Fear. *Something.*

I had never heard you say you couldn't keep going. Mobula rays, a breeze, hair in your face. *I need to lie down.* That phone call was when things changed—not Mexico, and not when the moths struck the window's screen the night you disappeared. By the hospital, it was too late. I could still tell you I loved you, could still take your hand, but we had already been in the After-Time: the readying. The thing I tried to plan for in Chimayo was happening. Taking your hand after this phone call meant something else entirely, and after the hospital even something different still.

You wanted your tinctures. You wanted to stop pursuing their experiments. You would change without another intervention, they told us.

We took you home. We put you to bed.

"Look!" you said. *Look.*

See also DEATH; FIX.

EINSTEIN, ALBERT (1879-1955) was a physicist and one of the most influential thinkers in the world. At five years of age, an encounter with a compass set him on a lifelong journey to understand the unseeable—the forces beyond our visible world. The mind behind the general and special theories of relativity, Einstein postulated time was relative to an observer's frame of reference and could vary from the frame of reference of another observer travelling at a different speed. Like Newton, Einstein believed the laws of physics governed time, but he did not accept that all bodies shared a universal absolute time.

I try pinpointing when the octopus arrived. Soon after you called with your news, doctors began referring to your tumors as "ink spots"—barely visible dots of pigment discovered during your routine procedure. I visualized a hot-tempered animal squirting melanin from the centers of its tentacles, its plum-colored lump of head bobbing inside your body. It became a distraction, a thing to focus on instead of the fear.

But then came more office visits, and days and nights preceding scans and biopsies, when that octopus would wrap itself around my insides with a ballerina's precision, a gentle strangulation, as I observed clinicians observing you. It kept me awake at night, kept my appetite at bay. During appointments, I took diligent notes as we sat looking seasick. The octopus twisted, lodged around my organs, one tentacle gently uncoiling to reach my throat, its sucker a knot in the ridge of my clavicle.

Maybe it appeared in the doctor's office, or maybe when you called with the news, or maybe it had been there all along: outside the frame of the image of you at the sea all those years ago, waiting for a future moment to arrive to drop into the both of us. I suppose the time at which it arrived doesn't really matter all that much anymore: it waits in my throat, still.

When his collaborator and friend, the engineer Michele Besso, died in 1955, Einstein wrote to Besso's family in condolence. "Now he has again preceded me a little in parting from this strange world. This has no importance. For people like us who believe in physics, the separation between past, present, and future has only the importance of an admittedly tenacious illusion."

Einstein died just over four weeks later.

See also MINKOWSKI SPACETIME.

ENCYCLOPEDIAS are books, organized alphabetically and comprehensively, covering an area or areas of knowledge. Lately I've conjured to mind those we kept in our apartment's hallway growing up—one material asset from the divorce, musty and pressed together on the bottom shelf of a cabinet, a row of *World Book Encyclopedia*s with spines bound in leatherette the color of worn baseballs. *B* for *body*, a five-page series of transparent images layering together the circulatory, digestive, reproductive, muscular, and nervous systems across a slick set of pages.

Once, when I was a child, you pointed to that page and said something like: *Here is the heart. Here are the muscles of your arm. This is like you, but alive.*

I fingered the embossed *B,* pulled the pages from one another: I was the skeleton on the page with no hair, teeth like unmarked dice. Kidneys in the shape of my grandmother's swimming pool. There was my set of ovaries, a trachea with a stem like a rooted plum tree. It was *like* me, I realized, but not alive. I could layer the pages to see my different parts, twisted inside. Everything was fixed, easy. The image on the page didn't have feelings—it wasn't sorrowful or lonely. It didn't ever have to find the right words because the words were already there beside its image, imprinted on the waxy paper, ready for taking.

Encyclopedias provide factual information, but they, like all texts, are authored, constructed so that subjects become captured. Things can be held under a magnifying glass one entry at a time, forever. Does that permanence give them a sort of truth that they are still existing? How, I wonder, does a writer account for the ways *time* is written into entries? Surely, definitions shift. Things change, and therefore so do *meanings*—but on the page, the words are impervious to adaptation, to learning. Maybe I can gain something from that sort of cataloguing now. After all, it was those books I went to so often back then, when I wanted to understand something.

In "The Plates of the Encyclopedia," Barthes describes how the first encyclopedia, constructed and edited by Jean le Rond d'Alembert and Denis Diderot between 1751 and 1772, put knowledge in one place. Though Barthes writes specifically of the *Encyclopédie*—a work composed of plates of images—he remarks on the magical quality of the structure to present objects in ways that are both highly variable and fixed on the page at once. He notes an enlarged flea becomes, to the reader, a monster; a snowflake, a flower on the page forever. The object, he wrote, "…is thus accounted for in all its categories: sometimes it *is*, sometimes it is *made*, sometimes it even *makes.*" The encyclopedia, then, can stop time. It makes poems, Barthes says, out of ordinary things. A snowflake becomes a *flower.*

What will I remember in five years? In twenty? I am afraid of forgetting the exact way you looked with your mouth open to the snow in Seattle, each snowflake a flower falling in your mouth. "Sometimes, very briefly," Barthes wrote of his mother, "a blank moment—a kind of numbness—which is not a moment of forgetfulness. This terrifies me."

I'm left with so many questions, like: How will I find you? Will you return? What role will time play in altering my relationship to you in the past, the present and future—in the After Being?

—Yes, an encyclopedia can help with this. It can explain things you may no longer understand.

It will keep our things safe—it will keep them forever.

See also ENTRY; EVERYTHING.

ENDINGS. *Come to a bad end. End of the rope. End in tears. Tail end. Dead end. Never end. Upend.*

I tried these words on when I called people who loved you. I fumbled with them. *She passed*, I said in a letter to friends. I meant *you*. You were now the *she* in reference. I found something very comforting about letting your phone stay on next to mine, Horoscope.com, Southwest Airlines, robo-callers all unaware of what had transpired. *They* thought you were still here. Their text messages and emails continued to light the screen and I told myself if the screen lit, that meant you were still here.

An ending is the final part of a period of time or story. In reference to space, it composes the limit or one final point. Think: terminate, close, maximum, conclude. Seas are bordered, though they appear endless—but how does a thing with fixed sides cease? If a wave never really dies, if it only recycles in on itself, how does it finish, and *to* where exactly does it go? When an episode, book, or play ends, I shift myself in some way. I turn the channel. I close the cover and vacate my seat. But this kind of coda is so unfamiliar. Where exactly is your end—*our* end—if you were here and then not, but I still try keeping you alive in some way? In the times when you were here, conclusions were parts of stories I evaluated and considered only in relation to what had come before. Now I'm not certain where the end even is—or if there *was* an ending, especially if I can keep your phone on, especially if I can find ways to trick myself into believing you are just unavailable.

The start of endings, sometimes referred to as denouements, are moments of the final unraveling of the plot, where the final solution is made clear for the reader. Accomplished through res-olution, an unexpected plot twist, or experimental approaches which break the rules altogether, endings often drive home the symbols, themes and deeper meaning of the story.

The phone lit up. It kept lighting.

K, one message said to you. *Earn 1,200 Rapid Rewards Points with Budget.*

False endings are a device used to trick the reader into believ-ing the end has come, only to then surprise with a new plot fold.

You disappeared. Some would say that was the end. I laid awake. I recalled my fingers on the thin pages of the *World Book.*

What about time? Barthes did not write to his mother, he wrote *about* her. He says he takes the work of grieving into the work of writing because it is the only way to come out of the loss, but I wonder if he really believed that, or if that note was only a construction of hope he was attempting to manifest.

See also OTHER SIDE; QUANTUM LEAP.

ENTRY. Writing to make sense of us can both compress and sup-press time. What *really* are Between Times, borders, crystals? There is also the Ronco Electric Food Dehydrator, Home Depot, tarot. Barthes says in "The Plates of the Encyclopedia" of the image of a man reduced to a network of veins, "*What is it?* What name to give it? How give a name?" The snowflake becomes a flower, but what about your altars, carwashes?

Once, during my first year away from home, you sent a birth-day gift to my campus address. I received a notice in my P.O. box to claim it, but when I went to the post office window, the package couldn't be located.

"Did you get your present?" you asked on the phone.

I explained it had disappeared. "Don't worry," I said. "It will turn up."

I returned to the window each week to check, but the box went on missing and you continued agonizing.

"But your birthday gifts are inside," you repeated, "and I sent two rolls of quarters for laundry!"

"I'll get other quarters, Mom. It's okay," I said. "It will turn up."

I never should have put money in the mail, you worried every time we talked. Money was always a worry.

This went on for months.

This is an entry about the time you sent something that never arrived. It shows how much you worried about helping me accomplish small tasks like laundry, even though I was over three hundred miles away and had attended to my own laundry for almost a decade by then—you had shown me how to pull a stepping stool to the machines so I could set the dials long before I was tall enough to reach them on my own.

How does this magnification change the entry's meaning now?

What about the part of the story when I went to the counter one last time, the week before the school year concluded and my address changed, and they presented the box they had found tucked far back on a shelf, wrapped in paper with your handwriting, sealed under neatly arranged strips of packing tape? Nestled inside were a pair of cotton pajamas stamped with flowers, a butterfly windchime, containers of my favorite peanut butter, and a package of gummy bears. The two rolls of quarters were enclosed in tissue. The birthday card was dated four months before.

When I called to say it had arrived you laughed, but then your voice trembled. You were crying.

"I'm just so happy it got there," you said. "I'm just so *relieved* it made it in time."

How does the meaning of this entry change now?

EVERYTHING. It would be so easy for this to become unwieldy: every tarot reading, each feather you set alongside an altar with a wish, all the moments we spent facing the television screen in repose. Quarter rolls for the laundromats. Sleeves of Chips Ahoy!. The way you folded the bathroom towels. How we were fused in a system of getting through each day—you and your work grind and extra jobs and me alone at home with the television while you and J worked, until I was old enough to have a job myself. Clipping persimmons from their branches in the autumn in your parents' orchard, slicing their pulpy flesh into quarters and sucking the seeds out—I would eat a million if I could find you in the row of trees now with their boughs down, their hefty weights. You at the end of a trench in your boots and apron reaching towards the sun, letting a shaft of light fall onto your hair.

This could be about you and the trees and every piece of fruit hanging from the limb pregnant with life and everything you said I still remember, but it can't be. I have to *choose* how to put you here—choose how to put *me* here *with* you, and which moments I want to fix on the page, forever. I will have to make decisions.

Your eyes. The way you folded the towels.

FINCH. A seed-eating bird, finches belong to the Fringillidae family. Small in size, they have beaks well-equipped for breaking apart nuts and fruit seeds. Finches played an important role in Charles Darwin's research of the effects of natural environments on biological evolution. We kept many as pets.

Do you remember when I found the first finch? A slash of color yellow as a pineapple wedge, affixed to the center of a manhole with its wing twisted back. I found that bird in the street in front of the house we all once lived in together, one weekend when J and I were visiting our father. My father provided a shoebox and lifted the bird off the ground in his hands, and I brought the bird home to you where it shivered on a folded-up paper towel.

Free as a bird. You said that when you talked about driving your old yellow convertible down the country roads. You said that when you talked about moving to Arizona.

We put the bird in a cage and set the cage in the kitchen. It was a small animal—I could cup it in one hand while making a hood to put over it with the other. The finch did not peep. It hopped back and forth between the wooden dowels. You worried the bird was lonely, so we bought another, and that finch made the other bird sing. They sang together. They built a nest inside a small rattan cup we fixed to one of the corners of the cage and soon it filled with a clutch of eggs, blue as forget-me-nots. When they hatched, five more birds peeped on the dowel. We observed them when we ate our toast in the mornings, and put a beach towel over the cage at night to quiet their stirrings.

In one photograph, you clip a coupon at the kitchen table where I twist around you. The cage sits on the fireplace behind the table, where the birds are trapped inside. My father must have known what would happen, putting the first bird in the box that day: you gave so much care tending them every day, repairing their small nests, folding fresh newspaper into squares to line the cage's bottom.

But you *did* contain them—we did that together. You were showing J and me tenderness, how to love something, but I do not remember when the birds were set free, or how. I do not remember if you took us outside into a patch of dirt where the mustard flowers grew, to open the door of the cage. I do not remember if you said, as they each fluttered out, their bodies small flashes bright as coins in the sun, *Here: look. See how we're watching them leaving? This is how you see a beautiful thing go.*

One day, you brought home another cage. It filled with birds too.

FIX. *Can you fix it?* you'd ask about the television cable box, the Christmas tree stand, the toaster. You were busy working, busy on your own with two children, desperately trying to keep your head above water and make rent. We all had to pitch in to stay afloat. You'd leave a list on the kitchen counter and a blank check for the grocery shopping. At the bottom of the list would be another set of to-dos: *wash laundry, wipe down counters, fix the vacuum.* I was good at solving problems; I liked to learn how to do new things.

Fix the gate latch, fix the car clock, fix the knob on the bathroom door. The fixing of simple machines is no longer a task now—you won't be calling to say you can't log into your computer. How do I fix the problem of *this*—your not-being?

This wrestling with time, creating a shape, it is a *kind* of fixed.

You took your last breath at 4:40 p.m. on a Monday, eight days after we brought you home walking and talking, alive and able to kiss my face. The certificate of death states your hour of expiration as 6:15 p.m., a time fixed to a document that cannot be changed.

"She passed forty minutes ago," I told the hospice worker over the phone when I called like they told us to.

"She dies when I put eyes on her," the worker said, as if he could see things I could not.

What he meant was that you would be gone when he said you were, which was another problem with time—but if you didn't pass when you actually did, *had* you really? Could I not, like this stranger, put eyes on you when *I* determined? That language opened a portal where it became suddenly possible to convince myself you were perhaps not dead, exactly, just sort of disappeared—lost, in the folds of time.

It is possible, I know, that I was looking very carefully already, for a certain kind of invitation. I can admit that to myself.

"She is going to Hawaii next week," we told your team at the hospital, after we returned from Mexico, after they told us you should do things to make you happy.

"This is not a good idea," they said, gesturing to where you lay in your hospital gown, eating chicken nuggets from a plastic tray, the first food you'd had in days, taking back the thing they had just given you: hope. Or at least: time. Everyone had plans for you.

You didn't go to Hawaii, a place where 6:15 p.m. was two to three hours ahead from us depending on the time of year; time zones just more rules, like principles of physics. We wind our watches forward or backward when we travel; we accept these equations for time—but what if I didn't? What if the rules were just complicated numbers working on the page, but not, in fact, in reality?

Time folded in half: you were alive and then a stranger said you were not.

That phone call and moment in the hospital make it easy to pretend you're away in Arizona instead of gone—I can get by for days or weeks thinking so. B says this probably isn't healthy, that each time I'm forced to confront the facts, I put myself through the shock of your death again. Maybe he's right, but it serves as a mental flotation device. It is its own kind of fix for now.

In episode thirty-two when Sam stands in the cornfield threatening to quit, Al reminds him of what he's been presented with. He tells him he would do anything to see loved ones he's lost again—anything to get the chance Sam has in that mission.

In the end, Sam cooperates. At the Thanksgiving dinner table, he looks carefully at his family knowing he will lose them. Knowing he has lost them. *Is* lost.

I am having the opposite experience where you are nowhere, and the only way to will you back is with illusion—or, at least, *questions.* This gracelessness is just a kind of clinging. The fix only a lie I tell myself.

Do you remember when I stole the neighbor's doll clothes because she had so many things I wanted that we could not afford? You found me on the floor of my bedroom playing with them, and walked me back to say to her face exactly what I had done with her things.

Desire. Problem. Resolution.

To fix it, you made me look at what happened. That is how that story ended.

Who am I now?

See also QUANTUM MECHANICS.

FOG. The fog arrives in my postbox on a morning in July, the day after the moths beat against the window. They are now beating in my ears with the clanging sea. The mail has collected for many days while B and I were with you and the rest of our family. In the mail: an advertisement for a local restaurant, furniture catalogues, and Home Depot coupons initiated by the address change I registered just ten days before.

There is also a letter from a bank I don't patronize, addressed to my name, regarding defaulted accounts which have gone overdrawn. There are fees.

Upstairs in my apartment when I call, the customer helpline wants to know who I am. I tell them I am Kristin Keane, of course—the real one.

"The real one?" they ask.

"The one who belongs to the social security number, but not the one who opened the accounts," I say. "These aren't mine."

They want me to verify myself. The last two weeks have warped me into a different dimension; I don't know who I am now. A day ago, I had a mother—you. A day ago, two years after we learned you might, you disappeared. Just *yesterday* you lay beside the window. Outside: the persimmon orchard, the owl house. Now you are not here, but the trees still are.

They need information I don't have. I ask when the account was opened, when the whole thing began. They can't tell me, they say. They can only talk to the Kristin who opened the account.

"But I *am* Kristin," I tell them: "It's *me*."

"Who is 'me'?" they ask.

—

In the living room, where I attempt to verify exactly who I am over the phone, B's and my things are undone. Just ten days before, I had been packing for our upcoming move when the phone call came that you needed medical help. In that time, only books were packed, but the contents of the buffet spilled out waiting on the ground: wine glasses, a box of candies filled with chocolate liquor. A stack of napkins sewn by my mother-in-law. Left alone, the cat chewed on sheets of bubble wrap and they are on the floor, too. In the kitchen, taped to my computer monitor, are four images of us from a photobooth taken two summers before, on a trip our family took soon after your diagnosis: smiling, aghast, posing as animals. You kissing my face. *To the moon and Back,* you wrote on a note suspended above them, left on my computer on a morning you stayed with us during treatment. *2/20/19. My love for you. Mom.*

There is the heart you drew on the note. A rock carved into a star you left on my desk early that summer. A penny found on the asphalt where you parked outside my apartment building. They all are still there, collected on my desk—but *you* aren't here, on the first day of my life without you in it. You can't help with packing as planned. You won't see the house we worked so hard to own—a dream my entire life, and one I hoped to have ready as an option for you, a place to stay when the time came.

But it was already time. Time had happened yesterday. Time had happened the day you called to say they found *something.*

2/20/19. My love for you. Mom, written and stuck to my computer where light shined through the curtains, where for five months light passed through the curtains, fading the ink of the note. No light poured into the room now, only bewilderment, an obfuscation I could not see but could feel, entirely changing the meaning of what you wrote that day, just five months before.

See also HOME DEPOT.

FOLDS happen when something bends and covers another part of itself as sheets, napkins, newspapers, or arms do. The clothes in your dresser drawers were always perfectly organized, pressed at the hems. Plots *un*fold, meaning they become revealed to the reader in pieces.

I go to the bank branch to clear up the confusion with the mail. On the way, a debt collector calls my cell phone regarding a defaulted loan, though the only loan I have is the one I've been packing my life up for.

A man asks: "Is this Kristin?"

"Yes," I say.

He rattles off credentials, then numbers—he tells me to pay off the account or things will escalate. Stunned, I hang up. I pull out the photograph of you I had been keeping in the jockey box of my car for months. In it, you sit in a rattan chair, your skin honey-colored with summer, lips painted with a strawberry gloss, a gold *Olan Mills* emblem stamped into the corner: *1987*. You're my age then—thirty-eight. A crystal pendant hangs from your neck. This was when you'd begun experimenting with the afterlife, with tarot cards, having your aura read—your palms, your astrological charts. I would sit on the floor with Legos, building my sitcom set replicas, while you talked to psychics on the telephone. You smiled, just on the brink of finding yourself, spilling into what you hoped to be. You intentionally saturated yourself in time then, in its anticipations.

I can get through this, I think to myself. *I can't get through this.*

If Einstein said time was an illusion, what, then, are these moments surfacing: your smile, last breath, the post box, the bank teller? There was an order to this, wasn't there? Maybe the laws and math are wrong. Maybe they haven't evolved with each sorrow of the universe; they don't understand, as Barthes does, that snowflakes are really flowers when you examine them closely.

FOURTH DIMENSION. Three-dimensional geometric space is usually represented by the coordinate axes x, y and z, each perpendicular to the others. Four-dimensional space introduces an extra coordinate—represented often as w—which cannot be seen, exactly, but can be mathematically modeled and imagined. It goes side to side, up and down, and *also*—somewhere else—forming into conceptual objects such as tesseracts, which are analogs of three-dimensional cubes. Fourth dimensional geometry is hard to render. It's even harder to wrap the mind around.

This is a story that is told in reverse, about reversal, about making, about *un*-making. It starts at one kind of ending, then moves backwards. This story is a corpus, held together by strings of love, by themes, by memories. Surely it is missing parts.

No—this is not in reverse; it is flipped upside down. The beginning of this story was told in order, now it is focused on the experience of time in life without you: you were here on a Friday when you went to the hospital. You were here the following week when we took you home. By Monday, you were gone. The next day I learned someone had taken my name: the Mystery Kristin Keane. The order of events matters less now than the feeling of them: a Then Time memory emerging after a Between Time.

I am sorry if the way I'm constructing this story causes you to lose your bearings. I'm just not sure, actually, where things end or begin.

Your death became the flash point, the moment when I slipped away from myself, and drifted down your face into nowhere space, into a fog which is both literal and figurative. That is also a time-problem. This is where anticipating that you wouldn't be here and not understanding what you not being here would be like, has to be confronted. I have to make decisions to pretend you are in Arizona, or fully realize that in fact you are not. Where I have to make decisions about what memories to conjure, what entry points I can explore the insides of: finches, roses, lost mail, your hands.

This is a story about finding the meaning of the story.

No—this is a story about finding the lines between things after arriving in a space with formed borders where there had been none before: me on one side and you on another. Mystery Kristin Keane on one side, and me on another. The Before Me on one side, and the After Me on another. I'm not sure at this juncture which, exactly, is the central character.

There are memories now and that is all that is left.

Four-dimensional space introduces an extra coordinate—represented often as w—*which cannot be seen, exactly, but can be mathematically modeled and imagined. It goes side to side, up and down, and* also—*somewhere else—forming into conceptual objects such as tesseracts, which are analogs of three-dimensional cubes.*

Yes, I have this right, I think. Dizzied by watching you take your last breath, by how, immediately after that, the Mystery Kristin Keane inserted herself into my life, I begin to rely on the possibilities of the fourth dimension almost immediately, where in that space, we go on together always, reliving moments linked together across axes.

I begin spending a lot of time this way now, falling into time traps where I construct how the x's, y's, z's, and w's intersect at once and not at once: your birth, J's birth, my birth; you drive your first car; you graduate from high school; you make boxed cake and let us lick the batter from the hand mixers' ribs while we sun ourselves in the riverbed where we camp, our fingernails lined with dirt; J and I hang from rope swings, we sail through the air while you watch with your feet in the cold water and clap to us in mid-flight from a place we can be in forever with you; J marries in a meadow full of flowers while I marry B under the owl house in your parents' persimmon orchard, where we pick fruit with our bare hands; you fill a plastic swimming pool, its interior lined with sea animals, J's daughters—your granddaughters, my nieces—splash each other in the water, all your girls together, as you like to say; you laugh you are always laughing—the three of us can stand beside one another in the mirror of our apartment's bathroom in the '90s brushing our teeth, curling our hair beside the towels you neatly folded stuck there in the cabinet, there forever—there always at the same time, in the fourth dimension where no end comes. There is no you, disappeared, only a forever-folding.

"Look!" you said. *Look.*

See also MANY-WORLDS INTERPRETATION.

FRACTURE. When you began radiation in June, a small rock struck the middle of my windshield. Two-hour drives along major highways back and forth to you worked the pit into a line and then a bigger line. Each roundtrip stretched the crack farther across my window—it twisted; it turned into switchbacks. I decided that, given the circumstances, I would wait for a complete separation.

A few weeks after you disappeared, my father came to see our new house and we drove to breakfast. He looked at the windshield and asked when I would fix it. I had told myself this cleavage couldn't have been a coincidence during all this sorrow, that perhaps if I let it expand fully, some sort of trapdoor might reveal itself in the fissure and a new reality would emerge. This same kind of logic I used when roller skating as a child: avoiding a fracture in the concrete meant we could afford that Ronco Electric Food Dehydrator; if I hit it, we couldn't. The same kind of thinking motored the fantasy that you were just unavailable.

"Really?" I asked, "with all that's going on?" I thought about the Mystery Kristin Keane, about your cremains back at home in a room full of boxes.

He shrugged. "Seems like an important thing to fix," he said softly. I did not tell him about my illogical hope—he only wanted me to stay safe.

After we brought you home from the hospital, your best friend planned to cut your hair very short. I took your photograph in the persimmon trees before she came. You put on a dress—the olive green one lined with purple flowers. You rouged your cheeks. You combed your hair. In one photograph, you put your fingers into peace signs. In one photograph, you close your eyes and stand in the sun. In one photograph, you rest your forehead against your mother's. In the last photograph, you blow me a kiss.

I can't take your photograph anymore. Is that a fracture? I can't see you anymore.

There is a line now between you in that last image and me just imaging you altogether.

FREUD, SIGMUND (1856-1939). Best known as the father of psychotherapy, Freud developed concepts for clinical practices such as free association and transference. Some regard the case of "Anna O"—a woman experiencing acute symptoms related to the illness and death of her father—as the first exploration of psychoanalysis. Led by Joseph Breuer, a friend and colleague of Freud's, "the talking cure" became influential for Freud. Later, he relied on similar free-associative techniques to encourage patients to uncover unconscious preoccupations.

Sleeping became difficult the day you disappeared, the moths at the window my first night of disruption. Now when I'm able finally to drift off, my dreams come soundless: they are railroad tracks, endless seas; familiar locations turned sideways. I wait for you to arrive in my subconscious with open arms, to find me in the quiet hours of the night.

What does it mean that I can't dream you? One of your friends calls your appearance in hers "visiting," and everyone else seems to get to, except me. Freud acknowledges that dream interpretations are blemished by our memories; there is no certainty they have even occurred. "It is true that this doubt betrays the lack of an intellectual assurance, but our memory really knows no guarantees," he wrote in *The Interpretation of Dreams*, "and yet, much more often than is objectively justified, we yield to the pressure of lending credence to its statements." Yet: dreams emerge as a path toward you, which is one I cannot yet get on.

What is the difference between a dream and an imagining? Both, I suppose, can be traps.

My life flips completely over. I am opened and shut at once. Undone.

Maybe if I examine them more closely, I can unlatch the locks and find sleep again.

Trapdoors

Trapdoors are typically situated in concealed locations, in the ground or a wall, which open into an adjoining space. In one sense, they are a snare—a figurative trap which the deceived fall into—but also an escape their designer can use for hiding inside.

Trapdoors can work in our minds to psychologically transport us into other space-time dimensions through hallucinogens or even by sheer imagination. In *Quantum Leap*, Sam's fledgling amnesia confuses his pre- and post-leap memory in this way—but sometimes, recollections slip through the folds: the smell of a cornfield in November, a pheasant taking flight. These moments of recognition elate him, but also bring him to his knees in missing: at one point he examines a husk of corn, comforted he has arrived back home; in another he races through the fields, scorning the design of his leaping, the thing that puts what he's lost into stark relief.

Trapdoor Number One

My first memory: walking to preschool. In my hand, your hand. You hold my Get Along Gang lunch box, its six characters spilling from the clubhouse caboose on the illustrated image affixed to its plastic front, a red thermos clanging inside with the peanut butter sandwich you cut neatly into quarters.

Its trapdoor: the way your hands felt, opens onto the last time ours touched. The sonic wheeze and crash of the oxygen machine.

Trapdoor Number Two
The concrete rim of the apartment complex swimming pool, my face pressed against its hot surface; the way it sparkled. We lie adjacent to one another on beach towels stamped with sunsets, a '90s palette of pinks and browns. Baby oil shimmers over our bodies, pools at the seams of our bathing suits. A collection of leaves clog the vent of the swimming pool and bumblebees drown on their furry backs. A popsicle wrapper on the water, a plastic flotsam.

Its trapdoor: me, you and J in the sunshine drinking cold 7-Up, listening to the radio in a patch of dirt and weeds, opens onto the images of your organs stippled with melanoma deposits. The way the doctors said "ink spots" suggested they were only microscopic. Meaning, they seemed inconsequential. There was a math that involved time folding. First you were here, then you were not.

Trapdoor Number Three
The long glass cases filled with boxes of cosmetics, the silver racks dripping with faux costume jewelry, the long stretches of neatly vacuumed carpet inside J.C. Penny's. We walk the corridor of the mall on my dinner breaks from Macy's where, in the evenings after school, I fold ties and sell leather wallets wrapped in crisp tissue. At Taco Bell, we order bean burritos. We fill cellophane bags with sour watermelon rings at The Candy Stop. At the stationers, you wind the music boxes and we observe the cylinder turning, its teeth ribbing against the comb of the box producing those familiar notes of "Memory," a song that sometimes made you cry.

Its trapdoor: you walking me back to my department and saying goodbye, opens onto containers of applesauce. Mashed bananas. Tablespoons of water and chocolate pudding, a collection of medical supplies beside the bed.
See also KAPPA EFFECT.

GESTALT EMPTY CHAIR TECHNIQUE. A form of therapy related to Freudian psychoanalysis and Jacob Moreno's practice of "psychodrama," the empty chair technique can be used to treat forms of Persistent Complex Bereavement Disorder—cases in which the bereaved experience prolonged grief that impairs normal function. Diagnosis of the condition is achieved through evaluating whether the bereaved meets one of the following criteria for at least twelve months: yearning for the deceased, sorrow and emotional pain, preoccupation with the dead person, preoccupation with the conditions surrounding the death. At least six of the following additional symptoms must also occur: prolonged feelings of disbelief regarding the death, difficulty with accepting the death, avoidance of remembrances of the deceased, inability to recall positive experiences of the loved one, trouble trusting others, anger about the death, desire to join the deceased in death, feelings of loneliness or detachment, feelings of meaninglessness, difficulty planning for the future, self-blame regarding the death, diminishment of personal identity.

In the empty chair technique, the deceased person is brought to session through role reversal. The clinician asks the client to first talk to the empty chair as though the absent person sits in it, then asks the patient to move into the chair and speak *as* the absent person, at which point both the clinician and the patient gain important insight about the deceased and the bereaved, while the patient "sits in the chair" of the one that's missing.

Let's say for forty entries, I have addressed your empty chair. Let's say the encyclopedia is my chair. Let's say I try moving into the other seat:

> *I believed in spirits, angels, vibrations. I had my aura read; I communed with the dead. There are experiences Kristin hasn't had yet. I worried about her worrying all the time. Kristin might have believed in some way that if everything I said was true, then I would find a way to make myself visible to her again somehow—that I would show her a sign. Maybe there's a chance she's resentful of this, that I misled her in some way. "Don't spend your time in traps, my baby," I want to tell her, but she has always thought this sort of way. She stood at the sundial and contemplated the shadow cast along its concrete basin from where I watched from the window. She observed. She was always observing.*
>
> *She watched her stories packed neatly into thirty-minute segments of time. If it wasn't the television, then it was her face inside a book.*

"You have quite the imagination," I'd say to her.

"I know," she'd say. "I know."

She is trying to cram this experience into a structure it might not fit inside to better understand it, but she writes from a present time retrospectively, relying on memories and guilt to try to reconstruct time: my illness, my death. She has a hard time remembering the good things and wrestles memories as if she's in a bullfighting ring, struggling to determine who she is now, and what these events mean to her life.

She sits in the fog, day after day.

Kristin used to say, "I love you more," and I'd tell her that just wasn't possible. She couldn't understand this, though she thinks she can: she has never been a mother.

If I could tell her I loved her now to the moon and back, I would.

See also CAST.

GHOSTS. No one can really be certain of ghosts, but many believe they're real—apparitions or spirit-forms of dead people. In some stories, ghosts are fed, pleased, kept from returning with rage—the word's likely pre-Germanic origin is presumed to mean "fury" and "anger." Ghosts are a kind of person after the person. They come in various material states, but are often described or depicted as floating transparent substances.

When my father's mother died, you gestured toward the ceiling and explained she was with us when the lighting dimmed or a butterfly crossed our path. Sometimes I'd walk home from school in the afternoon to find you wandering our apartment with a roll of incense, sticks tied together with a small line of twine, marking the air of our rooms to cleanse them. A shell was cradled on a small wooden stand on the carpet of the living room floor, tails of smoke drifting away from the ashes resting at its bottom. Dreams weren't stories your mind told itself so much as messages from the dead; *your* grandmother, Mrs. K, coworkers' parents. You spoke with them in the morning at your bathroom mirror while you applied a coat of mascara to your eyelashes. You blessed dead animal spirits on the side of the road with a special signal, your five fingers shaped into an amalgam of a goodbye: a wave and a release.

No one ever asks whether ghosts die, or whether they have an after-afterlife. Can you hold a ghost—or be held by one? I am attempting to contain *you*—to contain *us*, and give form to the nebulous and disorienting experience of losing a mother. I have addressed you: a thing no longer here. Does this make me an ally to myself in this story? Or if I am you addressing *me* (myself), am I just my own opponent?

When they told us you wouldn't have much time, I thought: *When you die, how will I find you if this isn't a thing I believe in?* I dreamt of you emerging from your grave, soil spilling from your hands. These moments—*these* are Einstein's illusions; the things my imagination makes on its own. But our life together, our time and each day spilled on the ground since you disappeared, are here in the material world. This is not only my perception—it is quite literally what I have now.

A ghost is not just a specter, but an impression, a trace of something else. Some say they only leave Earth once everyone who knew them is gone too.

Sometime during a fall oncology appointment, you revealed you'd taken breaks from your oral therapy. The doctor raised her eyebrows and I tensed in my seat. You said you couldn't handle the itching—the edema nearly swelled your eyes shut. On the phone a week later, waves of frustration crashed in the pit of my stomach, an ocean churning with an animal's pulse.

"What are you thinking?" I asked.

You listened quietly and then fought back. Something shifted. The octopus peeled back and unfurled its tentacles one by one. It lengthened into me and yours did the same.

"I want to run away to the desert," you repeated, over and over.

I saw for the first time we were both no longer ourselves. Instead, we floated adrift in the sea on separate deflating rafts, clinging to the plastic seams with our knuckles turned white, gulping down saltwater alone in the dark while our own sea monsters circled us, each of us thinking only of the After Time.

I can't say sorry for that day anymore. I can't say I *didn't* understand, that all I felt was afraid and angry you refused doing the things I thought you should. How I looked to control something because I knew I couldn't stop time. I can only tell you about the octopus now in this way, that the conversation was my love boiling over. This realization starts haunting me in the late days of summer, just weeks after you disappeared. It haunts me at the bank, where the teller helps me sort out the mess. I explain my situation, the phone call from the collector and the letter to the Mystery Kristin Keane. Other tellers crowd at the screen which he swivels in my direction to review the account transactions paid to a storage facility and something called Loan-Confidant.

The teller calls for assistance. When he does, Kent from the fraud department wants to know why I didn't come in sooner. I say I didn't know.

"My mom was dying," I say. "She—*passed.*" I haven't used "died" yet. *We lost her,* I told her cousins, an old boyfriend over the phone.

Kent's voice cracks. He's sorry, he says. His mother is gone, too.

"Can you tell me," I ask, "when this account was opened?"

"Looks like February twentieth of this year."

To the moon and Back, 2/20/19—a morning when you were alone in our apartment and B and I were gone to work, the day after your fourth immunotherapy injection. In the treatment room, we bent small straws into cranberry juice boxes. We ate graham crackers.

"Take my photo," you'd said. You smiled with your nurse, hopeful the chemicals pumping into your veins would work. Surgery hadn't worked. Other medications hadn't worked. In just a few weeks we would get worse news. In the bathroom, I tried catching my breath. I didn't want you to see me cry, how I had to put my forehead against the wall to breathe.

If you are receiving chemotherapy, a sign above the toilet read, *FLUSH TWICE.*

GOBLETS are often used in church services and ceremonies, where they're referred to as chalices. In the Catholic faith, they're used for serving Communion after consecration by a church official. Soured by parochial schools, you determined to raise J and me free of religious instruction, though my father's mother felt differently, taking extra care to supply her own kind of church education on occasional Sunday mornings during adolescence. The congregants would take the Eucharist on their tongues before drinking from the gem-festooned goblet the priest held in his heavily ringed fingers. I liked how its consumption promised goodness.

The altar boys who were classmates intersected with the only artifacts I knew of God: the crucifix, the chalice, the wafer. I closed my eyes during prayers and dreamt of summer vacations—me, you, and J on the Norwegian cruise ships advertised between my soap operas and infomercials, our own home with a backyard to sun ourselves in. Now, I just work at imagining myself back on that hardwood pew trying to remember the messages about redemption and death I might have missed back then—something I can hold onto. Did I consider God? I must have. My grandmother pressed her knees into the pew and the altar hummed with the light from the stained glass windows. I can't remember if I asked myself if I was good. If I was doing the right thing. I only remember the wafer, the assurance of something that could not be seen.

There are other things besides these time-problems to sort out, like the metaphors. Is finding faith a theme in this story? Is this about salvation?

You kissed me on the face and said you loved me, and that was the last thing I ever heard you say.

See also TRANSUBSTANTIATION.

GONE. When B leaves in the mornings, I am left with the fog. There is so much to do. I pack boxes slowly. Each room is cardboard and undone rolls of bubble wrap. I sit for hours at my desk gazing out the window thinking about Mexico. About you on the bed. Your last breath. I replay all the things I could have done better. *Stop ruminating, Kristin. Stop torturing yourself*, you'd say. I am alone with your cellphone. I call it with my own so I can see your name appear on the screen. I hold both phones at my ears.

Hello? I say to myself.

In one room, I find a photograph of you in a box. We had traveled to Cabo San Lucas once, ten years before—we walked along a pier one afternoon when our cruise ship docked in the port; a gift-trip J and I gave you for your sixtieth birthday. In the little shops, you filled your straw tote bag with knickknacks, small wooden figurines painted in red and blue. You bought a hat. At a restaurant we ate tacos, drank beer and birdbath margaritas salted at the rims. I took a photograph of you in front of a statue.

You are there in the photograph, but you are not here.

Time folds, but I can't remember what you said that day or if you touched my hair. I only remember the shopping and the food and the photograph. Why can I remember the sheen of the food drippings on my fingertips, but I can't remember what you said while we sat together?

Time has already shifted me. If all I'm doing is fooling myself by saying I have memories I don't really have, then what really is there left of you?

"Look!" you said. *Look.*

HAWKING, STEPHEN (1942-2018) was one of the most influential thinkers of the twentieth and twenty-first centuries. A theoretical physicist, Hawking is best known for his popular work *A Brief History of Time*, documenting the origins of the universe with an overview of cosmological theory—black holes, worm holes, the arrows of time.

I took your photograph in the orchard: you were standing, and you were smiling. Then, after one week of radiation, I arrived unexpectedly; you hadn't answered my phone calls in over a day. You sat on the bed crying, strands of your honey-colored hair on the pillows, the sheets, on your shoulders and in your hands.

You said, "This is horrible."

I held you like a baby. Why did I hold you like a baby? I did not know what else to do.

Here is something I do not understand about a theory referred to as *Hawking's Radiation*: near the edge of a black hole, one half of a virtual particle pair can fall into it while the other half escapes. If the fallen has a negative mass energy, and gets smaller and smaller before it explodes, then what happens to the particle pair they were matched with? They escape into a kind of trapdoor, but the other half is gone. How, exactly, are they changed, and into what state?

See also FREUD, SIGMUND.

HOME. There is a curious possibility at the conclusion of *Alice in Wonderland*, when Alice finds herself in a chair, awakened as if from a dream by her mother, that Alice exists in both the worlds of Wonderland *and* her home. As she turns to leave the room, the characters she's met along the way appear in the living room mirror.

"Can you hear us?" they ask. "Can you see us?"

She has become something else even though she found her way back home, and seems to be the same person—even though the viewer cannot be certain she's actually *made* it home, or if she is in another dimension, a multiverse where one version of her goes on in a place which *appears* identical. Alice's preoccupation with home dominates the entire narrative, yet we can't be certain it gets resolved by the conclusion, prompting the viewer to consider what home even means. If a place has the identical artifice of home, is that enough?

We made our homes in the rooms of a family member's home, then in apartments with mustard-colored shag carpeting and long bathroom mirrors. Everywhere we went, so did your altars: dried dragonfly wings, small mirrors, tarot cards. You pinned images of mermaids and wizards onto the walls; we built capsules of time together that way.

By the '90s, I spent entire summers in front of the television while you and J worked, watching show after show on our large hand-me-down Panasonic. Sitcoms became available via radio in 1926 and later became popular on television in the 1940s. Not all critics agree on the components of "situational comedies"—some say filming with a live studio audience or using a laugh track is an essential criterion. In the United States, sitcoms typically run episodically in twenty-two-minute-long segments to allow for advertisements during half-hour blocks of time, usually with a cast of consistent characters.

"You watch too much television," you'd say, snapping it off in the evening when you returned home from work: me on the floor with my face nearly pressed to the glass of the screen, as if I were trying to put myself inside it.

But the stories instructed me about character development, setting, arc, metaphor—they taught me that the elements of stories were everything. Soap operas taught me about interpreting people's calculated motives, gameshows about ramping up the stakes, establishing tension for the viewer when it became clear there was something to lose. Television supplied reliable lessons on recurring themes: coming of age (*The Facts of Life, Out of This World,* and *The Wonder Years*), the illusion of power (*Lifestyles of the Rich and Famous* and *Magnum, P.I.*) redemption (*Dear John, Unsolved Mysteries,* and *Cheers*), ambition (*Star Search, Fame,* and *American Gladiators*). *M*A*S*H* and *Miami Vice* built engaging, plot-driven story-worlds while *Coach, Highway to Heaven,* and *Family Ties* stressed the importance of lesson, the character's journey.

I climbed inside these programs, relishing everything in their tapestries—studying revelations about the human experience or a story's mechanisms—I delighted especially in reruns, the repetition. Family sitcoms were particularly satisfying—a predictable formula, an arc where even stories with elements of hardship resolved in happy endings—*The Hogan Family, My Two Dads, Punky Brewster, Empty Nest, Growing Pains, Mr. Belvedere, Charles in Charge, Silver Spoons.*

Home was formerly conceived of the place *you* are, with missing appearing to connect to the idea of location. How do I reconcile this if the disappeared object is now placed in an unknowable setting?

See also CHILDHOOD.

HOMESICKNESS is a form of anxiety reflecting the sufferer's longing for and attachment to home. In leaving you, I'd often develop painful stomachaches I now realize were a kind of separation anxiety. At sleepovers, friends' parents drove me home in the late evenings when I became melancholy, sick to my stomach with missing and worry. The first months away at college felt nearly unbearable, the familiar flutter of sick in my body returning always within days of visiting you on short weekends home.

With you gone now, the familiar biliousness of those times sets itself back in my body: a knot at my middle, a panic in my throat. But *this* time, there is no *you* to return to. What exactly, then, am I sick for?

"One minute you won't be able to talk to me anymore," you said, the two of us lying in bed, side by side, not knowing we only had fourteen more days together. Barthes wrote about his mother: "In the sentence 'She's no longer suffering,' to what, to whom does 'she' refer? What does that present tense mean?" Is it the breath that separates the past from present tense, or material existence—and in what form and until when—does that existence, exist? There would be no time left for us to occupy the same residence; you were not here, heavy with breathing, the skin recessing from your face. You were gone. Home was gone.

Yes, the *tense* has shifted: you are not 'is' but 'were.' You and your death in the Before Times is *past*.

HOME DEPOT. Just days after you disappeared, I roam Home Depot, searching for supplies for B's and my move. I like the way the shelves stack with unfamiliar products—caulking guns, furniture hooks, circular blades the size of dinner plates. Concrete mix, gardening shears, lumber, hammers. A haven of orange construction buckets, rows of shrink-wrapped rags, bays stuffed full with lumber, showroom doors, neat squares of carpeting, glassy washing machines.

At Home Depot, there is no ghost of you.

I walk the aisles like the crack in my windshield—in switchbacks. Among the orange-on-black and snaps of measuring tapes, the waxy leaves of the potted fiddle figs, I can hide. Lose time. I can stand in the elevator shaft and fall into a trapdoor just like I did with the fog: you don't need me anymore and now I'm in a nowhere space.

In the parking lot, as I turn plants on their sides, spilling handfuls of wet soil onto my car's upholstery, a woman approaches me pushing a small basket filled with cleaning supplies and rolls of paper towels.

"My mother loved rubber plants," she says to my back.

I turn. She's only a foot away from the car door, shading her eyes with her hands, close enough that if she tipped forward, we would touch.

"She passed in March," she says.

"So did mine," I say. "But … recently."

She smiles. "Who knew there were so many stages of grief?"

I look at my shoes.

"I feel like I'm in a fog of missing her," she says. She starts to cry.

I put my hands in my pockets and squeeze the teeth of my car keys.

"Yes, the fog," I say to the ground, wondering if I am this woman, if somehow *she* is the Mystery Kristin Keane. I want to take her by the shoulders, look into her eyes. *Are you, you?* I want to ask. *Are you the real me?*

She reaches out to touch my cheek. "Take care of yourself, baby," she says. She pushes her cart in the direction of the bus stop.

Inside my car, I pull the photograph of you from the jockey box—the one in the rattan chair.

Where did you go? I ask the picture of you that is not you. *Is part of me there with you?*

I drive through the parking lot and around the block where I see the woman waiting at the bus stop. I swallow, steady my breathing. She was not an apparition and I was not hallucinating: she is not another me. Barthes says in *Mourning Diary* that all things return as capital-F fiction, a reality I'm learning. This is the new space you and I occupy together now, where I'm left with your photograph searching for you—trying to will you back. You, inconceivably, are nowhere. You who always called me *baby*.

Home Depot as a Kind of Obfuscation

I wonder what the Mystery Kristin Keane felt like that day at the bank, the same branch I visited—opening the account and making herself into another me. What photo did she choose for her false identification card with my address and name—and had her mother taken it? And where *was* her mother that day in February when her daughter pretended to be someone else, a person whose own mother was declining, who just the day before, slowly unraveled inside a bathroom stall down that very same street, where *her* mother sat plugged into a machine.

I've been in a Twilight Zone, I write to a friend just days after you disappeared.

He replies, *That very surreal foggy feeling of trying to make sense of the day to day. In my experience it was such a torrent of swirling emotions that constantly changed on me.*

Each morning I have to remind myself I cannot call you—your phone is on my dresser, which means you won't pick it up. *Should I have left it in your apartment so you can call me when you come back?*, I wonder. Without thinking, I check my calendar for your next doctor's appointment.

I stumble into things, crash my knees against the toilet bowl, the end of the bed frame. I walk into a door, bruising my entire shoulder. While carrying boxes to the car, I trip and fall on the concrete nearly chipping my front teeth. I keep packing. I go the new house, make lists of the things we need. I think of the elevator shaft at Home Depot. There is not a fog around me, really—it is a metaphor for what is on the *inside*. It takes up hours at a time.

Home Depot as a Kind of Rationalization

B keeps asking if this is a good idea, all this change at once. There is a lot to do. I have to file paperwork with the Federal Trade Commission, freeze my credit, contact *those* banks, *my* banks, our new loan provider, figure out how to reach Loan-Confidant, whose customer service is an online auto-responder: there is no phone number. There are also your affairs—closing accounts, notarizing, mailing, J and I tracking down people who loved you.

I make other lists. Time collapses and expands: so much has happened in so few days.

"Yes," I tell him. "This is a *perfect* idea." Everything we need is at Home Depot, I say, as he looks at me skeptically. I visualize the ordered shelves, the calming wheeze of the air conditioning.

I turn the house upside down, feverishly packing each cabinet—discarding expired jars of gummy vitamins, ointments. I fill donation boxes with old coffee mugs and try to let the summer fog stretching across the city keep you out, but you are nowhere and everywhere at once. At the bottom of the utensil drawer: a heart-shaped spoon you sent as a Valentine. In the medicine cabinet: a dropper full of CBD oil you mailed for menstrual cramps. I pull the photo strip off of my computer and turn it over inside a box so I can't see our faces, tanned with sunshine. I feel strangled.

Friends come over to help. They look at me and cry.

"I'm fine, I'm fine, I'm fine," I say, like an automaton. I keep putting my forehead against the wall to breathe. I think of the elevator shaft.

Home Depot as a Kind of Church

Next, we move to the new house; to the fog. Near the beach, the fog waits all the time—in the morning descending instead of greeting, present when we open our eyes, tumbling across the stretch of backyards. Fog is often described as a blanket, but here it is an aerosol; the deck is sprayed until soggy, the plants in the backyard are wet all over with it. At the beach, sometimes the seagulls launch from the camel-colored sand into the sky and immediately vanish.

I put my whole self into it; days are shifted around, hours turn on their heads.

In the interim, I walk the aisles at Home Depot. I long for the permanence of the *Family Ties* living room. I long for your altars and your glass boxes.

At night I lie awake, illogically worrying if you'll find me in all these clouds once you return, at an address you don't know. I wonder: if this story was told from *your* point of view, would the complication of finding *me* be the central issue? This of course raises the issue of how a disappeared person constructs a storyline. Perhaps the dimension you're in now—perhaps controlled by an unknown math—is story-less, an idea which is about as difficult to grasp as you not being.

See also CHRONOLOGY.

HOROLOGY. Referring to the science of measuring time, horologists are responsible for manufacturing watches. Time piece features are referred to as *complications*, and include additional displays, such as dates or winding accoutrements. Watches with more than one complex feature are considered to have *grand complications*. Limited edition pieces manufactured to include aerial and cosmological features are referred to as *ultra* or *super complicated*—their movements, the mechanisms inside of watch casings, are among the most difficult to build and maintain. Watchmakers use loupes to look carefully at each piece, and tweezers to push around and remove small components, working through the complications like knots. Horology is often concerned with the engineering side of the enterprise—the actual dismemberment and reconstruction—but it requires a certain kind of meditation, a commitment to the act and responsibility of good time-keeping.

By early fall, several of my friends are pregnant, measuring their fetus's growth on cell phone apps which report their commensurate fruit size.

What fruit are you? they ask each other in text messages. *Are you an apple yet? A pear?* I look at my stomach wondering about what I'm growing and how to describe the size of the losing—oblong like a watermelon? Pitted as a cantaloupe? Time is getting them closer to something beautiful, while it only takes me further away. Perhaps my fruit is a coconut-sized appendage forming on the back of my throat where language emerges, full of nothing-space: every time I try articulating the way I feel aloud, the octopus appears, possibly rooting itself there permanently now, as if my throat were a crevasse in the sea.

But missing cannot be represented by nectarines. It fills rooms, transcends sheetrock, concrete. It is an uncontained shapeshifter, sucking everything else inside it, a kind of black hole collapsing my sorrows in such a way that light cannot shine back in. The thing growing in me has no breath, but is as strong as a thousand clock hands, each tick a reminder that me and my memory are gaining more distance from you. I need a meta-time, a thing fueled by the kind of heartbeat I desire—one that is rule-breaking, empathetic, aware of its power enough to offer some kind of mercy.

In DC Comics, there is a concept called hypertime, an in-universe framework formulated as a diagram, making the timelines of stories accurate, even without continuity across existing collections of storylines. The idea postulates a kind of multiversal transit map where each line, representing its own story, runs parallel, crosses over others, and carries on, with characters hopping from one train to another across universes. A reader in the third-dimensional space can look down and make meaning of the stories between the pages, leaving room for the possibility of a fourth-dimensional, hyper-cubic reader who examines that space, a geometric vision incorporating our universe along with the comic story world.

If I could twist time to my own design—if I drew it out in lines and gave it a taxonomy linking and collapsing all stories of the past, present, and future with all creators and readers—I would give that to you. I would give it a legitimate form, measure it.

INERTIAL FRAME OF REFERENCE. In a frame of reference not undergoing acceleration, Isaac Newton's first law of motion is valid: an object at rest will remain at rest, and an object in motion will remain in motion, as long as no external force acts on it. Meaning—without intervention, a thing left alone will continue do to the thing it does. A non-inertial frame does not obey this principle.

Here is an exercise I use: I wait on the floor at the sliding glass door in the morning and watch the fog. The rosemary bush and shrub blushed with blossoms are dewed by the morning. Sometimes a hummingbird vibrates nearby, sometimes a dragonfly. The sheen of their iridescence flashes in rainbows. A sheet of fog slips in, obfuscating pigment, and then it is just me and the gray and the reflection of myself in the window's glass.

Time folds. You were here, then you were not. I'm not sure what communicating with you means anymore. How do I relate the measurement of what has happened in my frame to what has happened in yours?

I pretend you are inside the room.

"Hello," I say.

I try imagining you sitting with me on the floor. "Hello," I say. "Hello."

I try to imagine your hair, your eyes, your hands. I try putting you near me.

The only thing I wrote down during the short period of time between Mexico and your disappearance was the following: *When you wrote my name today, you malformed the second 'i.' The 'i' you insisted on, the 'i' most everyone makes an 'e.' We spent an entire summer searching for one of those name plates children affixed to the fronts of their bicycles, spelled just like mine. That was before the internet. The two of us could probably find it now, but I don't think we have enough time. The rest of your letters were formed like a preschooler's—a sideways 'n,' a crooked 't.'* I took a picture of the way you wrote my name on the water bottle's label. I don't know why. I was startled, scared: your handwriting had always been so carefully formed. I thought if I took a photograph, then maybe I could put that moment inside its own container where it couldn't contaminate everything else.

"Hello," I say.

I reach for the picture of you on the altar I've built.

"Hello," I say.

"Who am I?" I ask.

There is the fog, a butterfly. I am waiting for a specter. I am waiting on magic. I am learning the difference between believing in something and relying on it. I am learning about how time moves forward, accelerating or decelerating whether I want it to or not.

See also JADE.

INSOMNIA makes it difficult to fall or stay asleep and can make the nighttime feel endless. Acute insomnia takes place over many days or weeks, but chronic insomnia lasts months or even years. Sleepless nights can leave one fatigued, irritable, "foggy," unable to complete normal personal and work-related activities. Insomnia—which in Latin means "without sleep"—occurs regularly for adults who have disrupted schedules, irregular sleep habits, related medical conditions, or, most commonly, concern and stress related to moving, finances, work, family, or the death of a loved one.

When I can't sleep, I think about the Mystery Kristin Keane. I wonder where she is while I lie awake sweated in a mess of sheets, listening to the night birds. Does she know I have moved, or does she still use my old address? It is interesting, I think, how much control she has, how much she knows about me—yet she is ghost-like, toppling over parts of my life so quietly, like a wraith.

When I can't sleep, I think about what it means to be able to not remember one thing, but not forget another. Is there a word for that—for the confounding nature of that experience? I can't forget the tear sliding from your eye, but I can't *remember* what you said to me at lunch that day in Mexico.

I think about Loan-Confidant, how I can't reach anyone. I write to say there is no way to call, that I don't actually have an account. I tell them about the fraudulent bank account the loan is associated with, how I've filed a report with the Federal Trade Commission so I won't be liable. I tell them about the debt collector, but their responses are literal zeros, as if they are a message in themselves. As if the response to my request for help is simply: no. I shout for help into the void, but the void does not respond.

Finally, my dreams change. You come, but now you're always back from the dead.

I'm sick again, you say, which is code for: we're going to endure this once more. This is the story my brain believes about time. "I am suffering from the *fear of what has happened,*" Barthes writes about the nightmares he has about his mother soon after her death.

In one dream, I wait inside a casino for a kind of healing ice cream in an hours-long line. When I try calling to say I haven't forgotten about you and about all the time we now have to share with one another—and yes, to say I *am* thinking of all the things I want to ask, now that I know I have the chance—you are no longer listed in my phone's contacts, and I can't remember your number.

Then, I run to you as I always do in these new dreams—abandoning the waiting to attempt to finally be with you again. But there are the long casino halls, a disorienting, maze-like carpet pattern, the fact I have remembered suddenly about a flight I need to catch. *I will cancel the flight*, I tell myself. It is more important to be here with you now.

It is always the same: you have disappeared and now you are dying again and I am trying to get to you, tied up with my life. It is not *you* repeating this, I know. It's me, telling myself I didn't do enough even though I attended the doctor's appointments, the treatments, the end. Even though I made you soup, made up beds for you week after week when you came to stay to try to get better.

Stop doing this to yourself, B says, except I can't.

What I *didn't* do was stop time; immobilize the force of the clock hands from doing what they did to us. Instead, now, I am the punisher and the punished all at once.

The running in the dream is not a metaphor for trying to find you—I am actually trying to do that. But can I anymore if you're not even here? You keep returning because I'm trying to give myself a chance I know I will never have, to untangle some part of that. That is literal, too.

INSPECT. On the beach, a seal lies bare on the sand with a hole in its face. Sand flies hum in a throng around its ears.

"Are you crying?" B asks. He puts his arm around me.

The person I loved first had a body that swallowed itself. I think there might be a certain amount of desiccated raccoons, beached animals, withered birds which can replace the visions of those last moments. That maybe instead of retracting my gaze, I can look enough so they will eventually neutralize what I've seen.

I determine that maybe the After Time Kristin Keane needs to rearrange herself somehow, cross the threshold the Mystery Kristin Keane crossed, where one cares less, takes what doesn't belong to them because they have figured out how. Maybe that hardening—not caring that time hasn't stopped for the animal washed ashore—will help me move through this experience, a sort of strategy to keep me from going under.

Animals—maybe that is the thing I need to understand. I need to think of you and I more as animals, so I feel less. I need to tell myself: it is normal for a mother to disappear; it is not normal to take it so roughly.

When we go through your things, a box in your closet contains a hummingbird wrapped in tissue paper. I expected watches, costume jewelry, but the hummingbird's eye is a withered bead, frozen in time and dehydrated just like the roses. You are not there in your apartment in the place I curled beside you on the bed, where you made tea while your cat circled your feet. But the *bird* is. The bird died long before you vanished, but it is there in the box just waiting for something.

Dreams can be inspected; so can texts and behavior. "Spectre" (meaning ghost) comes from "spectrum" which also comes from "specere" which also means to see.

"Look!" you said. *Look.*

JADE is a kind of stone, but one can also become jaded by repetitious efforts at attempting something. Yoked oxen can become jaded from pulling a cart, for example, or a person when they've made many attempts to understand a concept or idea they keep failing to grasp.

Two months before you disappeared, at a casino in Jackson, you won a thousand-dollar slot machine payout on your sixty-ninth birthday. There is a photograph of you holding the ticket: your eyes sparkle, you're smiling. The next day, you didn't feel well.

The following weekend in Pacifica, B's mother organized for us to stay in a rental near the beach. You wanted to see the ocean but felt sluggish most of the weekend. We stayed indoors and worked on a puzzle, went to the strip mall and drank wine without you. We went to dinner without you.

"What time is it?" you asked from where you rested in bed.

"Is it morning?" you asked in the night.

Two weeks later, in Mexico, you watched the sea from the balcony where you sat feeling fatigued.

"Before we leave, I'd like to go down to the beach," you said.

J and I ate without you. We went to the pool without you.

We didn't go to the sea without you.

We never made it to the sea.

Remembering this gets me nowhere, but I can't stop recalling this fact in the quietest moments.

We didn't get her to the sea, I think in the shower, driving to an errand.

It wears me down.

We didn't get her to the sea.

See also INERTIAL FRAME OF REFERENCE.

JUMP. Cancer appears to jump from one organ into another. This is called metastasis, a complex process by which cancer cells move into other organs, different from the one they originated in, until they cascade and there is nothing that can be done to save the person the cancer grows inside of.

Another kind of jump is a time-leap—paths Sam in *Quantum Leap* and Jerry O'Connell in the late '90s series *Sliders* use to move through time periods. Carl Sagan, a famous cosmologist, suggested time leapers disguise themselves among us. He died of cancer in 1996, at the age of sixty-two, after a career which included sending the Pioneer plaques and Voyager Golden Records—the first physical messages—into space. The latter included one-hundred-fifteen encoded images and audio recordings of things like the surf, seashells, and the Golden Gate Bridge.

Before B and I moved, I ran the same five-mile route through Golden Gate Park for fourteen years. Week after week I tracked the same trees, intersections, park benches, the Conservatory of Flowers, the de Young Museum. I ran past the same statues, sometimes the same runners. Exiting our apartment building was like slipping into a time-permanence: years of a peculiarly predictable route. The last time I left from our apartment's doors to run, you had been gone four days.

Sixty blocks west, on my first run after moving, I turn into the same park from the opposite side, moving towards the place I used to run from. There is a slow, uphill path I slog through, but then at five hundredths of a mile past my usual turning point—a small bridge above a children's playground—my watch signals my halfway mileage: the new spot is the old spot, but from the opposite side.

It's like looking in a one-way mirror—like the first time Alice thinks she's returned home, only to discover she's still trapped on the other side. She shouts at her parents to look, *Help me, I'm here!* They reset their hair, put their coats on. *Mother!* she cries from the other side, but they can't see her. They walk away.

For the rest of the summer, I often find myself above the playground where mothers engage their children with small baskets of toys, a see-saw. For just one moment, I stand at the middle straddling the line between the one direction I know, and the other I am learning. This is not backwards, exactly—the way I'm heading—although it feels a bit like it. Several times I contemplate jumping off and breaking my legs, giving myself something else to think about, a different pain to grind my teeth against besides the missing. B worries after I trip and skid into a pile of gravel on the trail and skin my hands, so I do not tell him about the bridge. I was thinking of you when I stumbled.

I know you'll worry about the bridge, but it's only a thought. I only stop for a moment and look.

In the woods, Alice tells the White Queen she can't remember things before they happen. "That's a poor sort of memory that only works backward," the White Queen tells her.

Alice asks her what she remembers best, and the White Queen tells her the things which happened the week after next. It is unclear in this exchange whether the White Queen is clairvoyant, or if she lives in a sort of sandwiched time—like the way I feel now, drifting either backwards, or desiring only future memories of you I know I'll never have.

"Jam tomorrow, jam yesterday, but never, ever jam today," she tells Alice.

J and I used to sing to this part of the television adaptation with delight. I'd shake my hair like Carol Channing, we'd put our hands out, never for one moment while dancing considering how in the place from where you stood watching us, someday you'd be gone.

See also ALICE'S ADVENTURES IN WONDERLAND

KANT, IMMANUEL (1724-1804). Influenced by thinkers like Newton, Leibniz, and Hume, Kant believed human understanding shapes experience and provides space and time to organize and process the external world and incoming stimuli. "Space is not something objective and real," he wrote, "nor a substance, nor an accident, nor a relation; instead, it is subjective and ideal, and originates from the mind's nature in accord with a stable law as a scheme, as it were, for coordinating everything sensed externally." Meaning: reality is what the mind has constructed.

The mortuary sends an email with images of your fingerprints. Four BMPs situate parts of you into corners of images. I pretend not to notice the way it appears as if you rolled off the page. Lined clearly, each is like its own tiny corn maze.

On one, I zoom into the line between two friction ridges which form a kind of channel. I zoom, in and out, as if I walking through them. My ear hums, it churns a sea-churn. I magnify again: in, then back out before moving the image so the cursor sits on a ridge, and then magnify it until it fills the screen completely with black: one greased line of you I can step inside.

I try remembering holding your hand. I look at my hands.

"Hello," I say to my computer screen.

"I am trying to walk your lines," I say.

"Hello," I say.

Is *this* it—embodying a different reality? I need to think more about puzzles and clues and strategies for solving them.

In some ways, it is easier to conjure the Mystery Kristin Keane, the one I've never seen. Like you, she's everywhere now, in phone calls and letters and reports I file to try to absolve the debts she's created.

"Hello," I'd imagine saying to her from my window.

"Hello," she'd say back from the deck.

Letting herself in through the sliding-glass doors to where I wait for you in the mornings, she'd enter like she owned the place, clearly used to doing what she wants.

"You've made a difficult time more difficult," I'd tell her.

"I know," she'd say. She'd wander the room casually, pick up my things—*your* things. The long stretch of amethyst. A pair of owl feathers you found in the persimmon orchard I keep under a small pot of cactus.

"Excuse me—do you know what I'm dealing with here? I've spent so much time cleaning this up," I'd snap, trying to meet her gaze. "Are you listening? I've spent hours on the phone at the bank and post office—*days*—trying to make this right. I can't even get some of these people on the line to straighten things out!"

"Sounds stressful," she'd say, lackadaisically popping her chewing gum as she eyed my cat stretched across a chair.

"*Stressful?* Do you know how complicated it gets when someone has taken your name away? My mother just disappeared! This is a total fucking mess!"

She'd look at me then for the first time, finally, carefully considering me standing in her way.

"You couldn't possibly understand what that feels like," I'd say.

She'd look at her legs, the floor, then at the dried strip of mud across the toe of her running shoe. Stepping toward me for the first time since she stamped into the room, her expression would suddenly shift.

"Well, actually," she'd say into my eyes that are the same shade as hers. "I do."

See also ABSOLUTE TIME; CHANNEL.

KAPPA EFFECT. Scientists experimenting with time perception flashed two lights at varied time intervals and relative positions. Participants observing the flashes reported equivalent intervals as having taken longer even when the lights were farther apart. This confirmed the *kappa effect*—how one's sense of time, the duration of an event—is influenced and distorted by the perception of distance from the thing observed.

On the streetcar home from dinner one evening, red wine and garlic noodles slosh in my stomach. The neon lights and intersections smear into wet puddles on the asphalt outside, juxtaposing with the reflection of the interior of the train: an image of the woman across the aisle, the handrails, B, and me.

I wonder if I look like the kind of woman another woman impersonates, if I look like a motherless woman. Are the lines between my eyes—those spreading at the edges of my eyelids, the tension in my jaw from nights of clamping down, grinding my teeth against one another as I replay every sad moment leading up to seeing you last, visible? Can *you* see them?

One morning you forgot the word "empathy." You said:

"When you have—.When you have—.What is that word—?"

"Empathy?"

"That word …—what is that word? I can't remember it."

"Is it 'empathy,' Mom?"

"Dammit … it's right there; I can't find it. What is that word?"

"'Empathy,' Mom?"

"Yes, that's it. 'Empathy.'"

I didn't point out that it *was* right there; I had offered it. Sometimes during that period, I considered I was dreaming everything up, that you were only playing pretend. I know I will imagine more things, now. I know how my mind works.

I wonder if the Mystery Kristin Keane lies awake with insomnia considering if she could have done more to save her own mother—protected her somehow. Maybe, like me, she did all she could—she went to the appointments, asked questions, researched information—only now she sees holes, places where maybe the questions weren't quite right, where the treatment plans went wrong. Perhaps she thinks she didn't try hard enough. Then, maybe she goes even farther, contemplating how these questions matter, but are connected to a much larger problem: the sense of time.

Is the thing I ruminate about, *you*, your *death*, or me *observing* your death? Each possibility blinks off in a space where they refract one another. Hard to measure exactly, they are harder still to know their distance from each other, like the image of myself in the window and the puddles outside and the lights from the street signs bouncing off the glass.

The *Please Hold On* sign pings. It lights up red. We bump over Sunset Avenue and the moon over the ocean comes into view. *P-p-p-please hold o-o-o-on*, the announcement stammers—or does it? It seems a little bit in that moment, to be a request just too on the nose: some nights you are the signs and some nights you are the signs inside them.

I am loose inside a vacuum where even words are twisted out of shape.

"In relation to the systems which surround him, what is he?," Barthes asks. "Say an echo chamber: he reproduces the thoughts badly, he follows the words; he pays his visits, i.e., his respects, to vocabularies, he *invokes* notions, he rehearses them under a name; he makes use of this name as of an emblem (thereby practicing a kind of philosophical ideography) and this emblem dispenses him from following to its conclusion the system of which it is the signifier (which simply makes him a sign)."

Meaning: everything is and is not a message.

KNOT. Knotting ties and tangles two or more parts together. A knot may or may not be composed of a single material—such as the ends of the same shoelace, or a rope, or two clippings of yarn. A knot is defined by its complication. In knot theory, mathematicians study knots which cannot be undone because their ends are joined—including a smooth circle (an "unknot"), the clover-like trefoil knot, and billions of others so far documented. Knot theory also helps explain principles of quantum mechanics—the behavior of atomic and subatomic particles, which knot theorists investigate through geometrical visualizations to observe life inside quantum boundaries.

In the fourth dimension, knotted crossings may be unknotted. Must Plutarch consider the way his ship functions there, or do puzzles come completely undone in that space? You with your hands in the air praying for mercy, and me looking sadly on at the beach where I took your photograph, is really just one version of one dimension. Maybe when you put your hands up, they were not in invitation, but parenthesis. Instead of, *Look God, I am alive,* you said, *Here is where Kristin's story will be driven off the rails; this is where her inheritance begins.*

Perhaps existing in the fourth dimension would feel like watching reruns—where a permanence, a *forever*-ence of all moments we've shared lives on; a kind of anti-time in which we go back—we could sit on the sofa together watching—me with my hands over my eyes just like I did before.

Maybe a story in the third dimension is too limiting. Maybe I have the principles wrong, but I suppose in this version of the story, you cannot help with that.

"I've never been good at math, Kristin, you know that," you'd say.

So I keep designing its loops:

In the fourth dimension, we go on in that space, always. Your birth, J's birth, my birth at once and not at once: you take your first steps, your mother claps for you, your gold curls and arms outstretched as you reach for something to hold onto; you meet my father you fall in love you are wrapping our Christmas gifts in paper so carefully you make the patterns match where you put the tape down; I graduate from college and you hold a balloon shaped like a butterfly from a fold-up chair on the wet grass; you hold J's first daughter you kiss her hair you watch her try avocado; you clip persimmons from the trees in the orchard you bring them to my classroom to my students who have never tasted them before; you are watching from the doorway where J and I dance with Carol Channing where we sing with Alice; you smile you always smile—the three of us can sit beside one another eating pancakes for dinner, Sam in the background leaping into other bodies our fingers are sticky with syrup there at the table—there forever—there always at the same time in the fourth dimension where there is no end where puzzles always get solved, knots always unknotted. There is no you, disappeared.

See also HOROLOGY.

KÜBLER-ROSS, ELIZABETH (1926-2004). Building on work from John Bowlby and Eric Lindemann, psychiatrist Kübler-Ross popularized the "five stages of grief" theory in her 1969 international bestseller *On Death and Dying,* a text widely recognized for establishing grief as a distinct process to move through: denial and isolation to anger, anger to bargaining, bargaining to depression, depression to acceptance. Data published in this book were based on *patients'* experiences with dying—not the experiences of those left behind by others' deaths. Though Kübler-Ross made efforts later to address how the model applied to the bereaved in a less linear way, the five-stages model maintains ubiquity in popular culture.

The act of dying is not the same as the act of grieving a loved one's death, however, and this kind of rigid framework can stigmatize grieving which doesn't adhere to these fixed enactments. Since then, researchers have offered alternative frameworks. In George Bonanno's *The Other Side of Sadness*—a counter-text to the traditional grief model—he argues that bereavement isn't one-dimensional, and notes lack of evidence for discrete stages of mourning.

One evolutionary explanation for grief posits it as a side effect of attachment—an instinctive trait allowing us to survive with the help of others. Another explains how sadness and loss can lead to adaptive behaviors that are beneficial, such as avoiding dangers which previously led to others' deaths, or anticipating the pain of grief and therefore taking better care of others to avoid it.

Surely, I could have done something. There must have been a way to stop the progress of your disease. Surely, there was a way to stop time.

This is illogical, B tells me. So do friends. I did all I could do, they say, yet the unyielding self-reproach sustains; it is a knot I cannot unpuzzle.

In *Critique of Pure Reason*, Kant asks, *What can I know? What must I do? What can I hope?* He says only the observable world can be known. One should act morally; one should hope for a just God.

I watched you take your last breath—what is left for me to attempt to make sense of? I

think about the idea of a time machine again, how it could solve all of these problems.

If unreasonable guilt is a theme of this story, what is the setting? I have tangled so many time-threads here, I'm starting to lose track of my own sense-making. Perhaps the setting is illogical guilt, or perhaps it's four-dimensional guilt, or just the fourth dimension. I do know a setting exclusively in the Before Time, or in the After Time, is not quite right. Maybe it is in another world where the two of those are entangled, where a fourth variable is required: the *w*.

See also W.

LABOR refers to the act of giving birth, but also to exertion or work. You can labor at something like love, or a crop, or—unexpectedly—an absence.

Two weeks before you disappeared, we lay in bed together. The small spots on your skin, in the membranes of your tissue, in your liver, lungs, brain—they were erasing the material you, little nothing-spaces that would split us into different dimensions.

I asked you, even though I do not have children, "Tell me what to do when a baby cries."

You said, "Hold the baby, feed the baby, change the baby. If the baby has a fever, take it to the hospital. Sing to the baby."

I asked you, "What do I sing?"

"Sing 'Rock-a-bye Baby,'" you said. "Sing anything you'd like. Sing a song that makes you happy."

You said, "You always talked to yourself when you were a child, outside in the mustard grass. Long conversations of pretending. You would play the mother, but you also played the child."

LEIBNIZ, GOTTFRIED WILHELM (1646-1716). Best known as an innovator of the modern binary number system and differential calculus, Leibniz wrote extensively on metaphysics, theology, and history. His myriad works include essays, scholarly texts, and letters, though many have yet to be published.

In the principle of the identity of indiscernibles, Leibniz postulates that two distinct things cannot have the exact same properties, or else they would in fact be the same identical object, and one object cannot exist simultaneously in different locations. In *New Essays on Human Understanding*, Leibniz writes, "… although time and place (i.e., the relations to what lies outside) do distinguish for us things which we could not easily tell apart by reference to themselves alone, things are nevertheless distinguishable in themselves." Leibniz advocated against Newton's absolute theory, for the relational theory of time.

I have your long legs, the same chin. We share the same sense of self-deprecation. The act of laughing overwhelms the body. But my hair is dark, my skin freckled. My eyebrows are a very different kind of shape. I do not believe there are supernatural reasons for why the cells in your body shifted shape, that a dream in which you appear is a message to me from across the divide—at least, I didn't before. You grew me, and then put me outside of you—how are we so different that way—or were? How do I decide what to believe in now?

There is something in Leibniz's idea which appeals to me: that perhaps you *are* located somewhere else, since you can't be everywhere, as you said you would be, and still be the same you. (I am trying, after all, to decide what to call this feeling of not believing

I could see you again, with being so heartbroken I was right—to want so badly to be wrong.)

Am I angry you're not in the After Time as I believed you wouldn't be, or am I angry that somewhere in that expectation, I actually *did* hope I had your beliefs laid inside me? Or am I just angry at myself, resentful of my need to order, to make sense of a heartbreak?

I suppose I have found myself in the unfamiliar location of being so desperate to be with you again that I will attempt to bend anything to my logic.

LETTERS make up the alphabet and represent speech sounds (the letter *x* sounds like "eks"; the letter *y* sounds like "why"; the letter *z* like "zee") but they can also become immutable correspondences between writers. A sender composes, then waits for a response while the receiver evaluates whether or not to reply.

I spend a lot of time thinking about letters after your last breath. I compose a note to Loan-Confidant:

Hello –

I still have not received a response. Please confirm and forward any relevant documentation that this account was fraudulent and that I am not responsible for it in anyway. Please also confirm and send documentation that the collections agency has been contacted and I am released from liability.

Kristin

When J and I go through more of your things, every nook is ordered. Your dresser drawers. The bathroom cabinet. A basket beside your desk. The charging cords are wound together and secured with rubber bands, each drawer lined with small, neatly organized dividers, containing a series of tools: scissors, post-it notes, stickers. Your things in the closet are folded, tidy. Little organization is required beyond deciding what will be kept, and what will be given away.

Three days into radiation you sent J and me a text message asking if we wanted any of the belts hanging in your closet. You also offered a bag. A pause came, and then those familiar dots on the screen as you composed your next message, as if you were reading my interior thought: *Don't worry,* you said. *I'm not going anywhere.*

Why weren't you resting that day? Why did you clean out your closet if you thought you had more time? And why wasn't I there telling you not to spend it that way?

I hope to find a letter tucked somewhere. I want something to hold onto, directions for how to time-leap as we undo each drawer, unfold every pair of pants. Surely, you would have had a plan for me, some kind of message.

I take photographs of the room before we begin, because I want to be able to remember it as you left it: your altars, the notes taped inside the medicine cabinets reminding yourself to trust the universe, to lean in, to be patient. We pack up your things in a single day.

I find the hummingbird in a box with an eye like a glass bead, but I do not find what I am searching for.

Why wasn't I there that day as you evaluated reducing the number of things stacked in your closet, instead of letting your body rest? Because I was somewhere else, unaware that in this time later, I would continue to look back at that message and shake my head at all I did not yet understand.

I receive a reply from Loan-Confidant revealing just how fast I'm getting nowhere:

> We've escalated your issue to a specialized collections
> department in order to thoroughly investigate your issue
> and get back to you as soon as possible. We thank you in
> advance for your patience Kristin!

LUNGS. In humans, the left lung is smaller than the right to make space for the heart. A sac surrounds each lung and the two are separated by a lubricated pleural cavity, which prevents lobes from bumping against one another—a handy system for keeping everything contained and safe. Human embryos' lungs form in the fourth week of gestation, but they don't function to breathe in utero. The respiratory tract develops like a tree: bronchial buds emerge and branch off, bifurcating into other parts through morphogenesis. When the fetus drops in late pregnancy, the mother typically finds it easier to breathe as her own lungs become less compressed.

At birth, hormones, pressure from labor, and the force of an infant's cries remove fluids from the lungs and allow for the first breaths. That happened to you in 1950, and for me thirty-one years later. Lungs are susceptible to many kinds of disease.

When the cancer moved into your lungs, we didn't know there would only be months left together in this dimension. In the last weeks, this was the thing that gripped you; took your literal breath away. It had only been one month since Mexico, when one morning you could not get up.

"The cancer is everywhere," they told us at the hospital. They told us it was time to prepare for the end.

Birds' respiratory systems spread across their bodies in a blanket of tiny sacs within their bones. Some reptiles like snakes and lizards only have a right lung; the other is small or even missing. Like other land crabs, the coconut crab is equipped with lungs which are like a gill for air. After mating, females glue fertilized eggs to their undersides until they hatch and drop into the ocean, small baby plankton drifting with the current then resting finally on the sea floor where they find their shells. All the while, they search for a life raft to cling to—a floating log to grow on. They breathe underwater until they encounter land, at which point they access their lungs. These small miracles take time.

I wonder what the mother crab thinks when she parts with them. When she separates her body from their bodies, and drops them into the savage sea. She might not have the language to say goodbye, but she carries their eggshells on her for days, eating them piece by piece, each molecule of her offspring she still possesses, put back inside herself.

Prepare for the end. I'll never forget that conversation in the hallway of the hospital: how impossible a word could seem I had heard so many times before.

The End—capital 'E', the caption at the conclusion of so many of my stories.

See also LABOR.

MAGIC. Did I tell you what I saw the afternoon I watched David Blaine break the world record for breath-holding? How fascinated

I was with how he engaged his audience? You loved the idea of magic—the occult, sorcery, the supernatural. A poster of Merlin, the wizard, hung from the wall of your bedroom for years in the '90s. J and I found it rolled up neatly in your closet the day we packed up your things. In the image, his hand casts a spell at the viewer. There is something I find very frustrating about the illustration: him permanently on the brink of delivering something enchanted, yet never actually succeeding.

"Oh, silly girl, it's just a picture, Kristin! Just something fun," you would say now. "I see *promise* in it."

If you were here, I'd ask what you think the difference is between an act of magic and a miracle. I think a lot about that now: the line between them.

"I'm looking for a miracle," you said so many times in the year before you disappeared. I never showed you my tin from Chimayo.

Most theologians and philosophers concur that miracles defy nature—that is, they are physically impossible, and are therefore divine. Here, too, is where constructs get twisted—surviving the zip of a lightning strike and walking upright afterwards is commonly labeled as a miracle when, in fact, statisticians have long argued that perceivably unlikely events actually occur regularly because of the population's sheer size.

When I watch Blaine's feats now, I see something very different: yes, there is the play with the viewer, the law-bends—but *why*? To break that record, he attempted breathing through chemicals, studied pearl divers, positioned medical interventions in his body to help him breathe.

What might be considered miraculous can be a kind of ordinary—some as common as cancer, as common as octopuses, as common as a mother dying. What *is* extraordinary is floating above yourself, watching your soul bend into a new you because of something entirely out of your control, a death and a rebirth of a part of yourself.

"I believe in miracles," you said so many times. "Hope," you said, "is what I need."

MANY-WORLDS INTERPRETATION is one theory among many in quantum physics related to the Heisenberg uncertainty principle, which states that there are limits to the accuracy of measurements at the quantum level. For instance, the exact momentum and exact position of an object can never be known.

Also known as relative state formulation and the Everett interpretation, the many-worlds interpretation is driven by the idea that for every given action, all potential outcomes are realized and branch out from one another in myriad worlds we're not aware of. Parallel worlds never intersect.

Leibniz wrote that God chose the universe to exist because it was the best of all possible worlds, eliminating the idea of infinite universes altogether, but this idea doesn't account for trapdoors or whether this world *does* have a way to get to others that have not yet been found. His is a theory that relies on God, and not on imagination.

For a century, the Copenhagen interpretation—explaining why particles might behave in different ways—presupposed they exist in all their different states at once. Erwin Schrödinger's 1935 thought experiment sealed a cat in a box with a Geiger counter and radioactive material, theoretically proving the cat would be suspended in an unobservable dual state of being, at once alive *and* dead. You took your last breath at 4:40 p.m., but your time of expiration is listed as 6:15 p.m. on your certificate of death.

In the afternoons after school, *The Twilight Zone* ran in syndication, a double pack of black-and-white episodes. I'd sit in my grandmother's sunken living room with my hand in a bag of frosted animal cookies, the rainbow sprinkles shaken off in my lap while Rod Serling led me into each story of characters making sense of their strange realities. Episode twenty-one of the original series concerns parallel universes. First airing in 1960, "Mirror Image" centers on Millicent Barnes, a woman who meets an identical version of herself at a bus station. When she explains the idea of an alternative plane of existence to Paul, another character waiting for transport, he thinks she's become unspooled. But after she gets taken away from the depot by police, Paul discovers another man who appears to be his *own* doppelganger.

At night, when I can't fall asleep, I design our multiverses, a way to get to you in the anti-time.

Parallel World #1: You remarry and move to Arizona, tend a robust garden where plants and flowers grow towards the sun before pouring their colors back onto the earth. You pick them up with your hands and the dirt spills off.

You hold them up when I come to see you. *This is what I made for you*, you say. *Everything is so full of life, here. Everything blooms.*

Parallel World #2: When you visit me at the sea, we become different animals. This happens as soon as our feet meet the seam of the tide's edge. We dissolve into the sand, into the particles of water; sliding our bodies back to the place where you watched me swim with sea turtles from a rocky shore in Hawaii, a place we had never been together before.

As the turtles swim with us, we develop rigid backs and leathery flippers. We buoy ourselves in the current, which sweeps our bodies into kelp forests we drift lazily through. We develop the heavy eyes of sea turtles, their mosaicked skins. We roll the tops of our shells under us and sun our backsides in eddies which turn us like pinwheels. The sun, it never stops shining. Anything can happen in the parallel world: we can be animals who become other animals.

Parallel World #3: Sam Beckett arrives at 4:41 p.m. July twenty-second, putting you and everyone you love into the Project Accelerator and back to when you were alive. In this new place (which is back in time but also in a new kind of time), you lead us inside a forest where we dance in the moonlight and make flower crowns from dandelions. We hold séances to call your spirit back—the one that is gone in the other time—and we laugh because you are not gone! You are *here*—with *us*—dancing in the night! Pretending is just a joke we like to play to remind ourselves of how easy it is to shift time, of how much improved our lives are because we understand how to evade all of its mathematical principles.

Parallel World #4: Life as it was. You build the cactus garden you planned for in the Before Time. You fill the plastic pool for your granddaughters on weekends. They run their feet through the wet grass. You go to town to paint at the coffee shop in the evenings with your mother—my grandmother. You bring stems of miniature roses rubber-banded with wet paper towels to my home near the sea. We walk on the beach.

Hercules crushed the crab with the heel of his foot—that's all we know of cancer—a piece of trivia from your zodiac days. We do not know "mucosal melanoma." We do not learn together about ends. We do not become characters. I do not have to ask questions. I do not have to answer them. I do not need a literary device. I do not need a story arc to try to understand this thing that I never even have to make sense of.

MEMORIES. You cut peanut butter sandwiches into triangles. You folded clothing carefully: perfect creases in stacks of cotton underwear. You ordered things; clipped coupons perfectly at the perforated line, stacked them neatly before putting them together with a silver paperclip. You taped fortunes into the medicine cabinet, delighted in miniatures, glass birds. You were tender with animals and buried the mice, the hummingbirds, the other dead left on the porch by the cats. You listened. You spoke to yourself in the mirror, you rehearsed chores, steps, you articulated your heart aloud to yourself and did not care who heard you. You grew plants and trimmed them neatly at their joints—you grew new plants in your windowsill. You always brought gifts—things you found, small glittered rocks for pockets, bumps of agate. You lined your cabinets with paper towels. You did everything with such good care.

"Kristin, pick a color," you would say and a pair of green mittens would arrive in the mail, carefully folded in bubble wrap.

You were quiet and you were not quiet. You were discerning and you were unsure. You did not know how to be anything other than what you were, and you loved me the same way, never conditionally, always just as I was.

This missing: there is not a word to describe its choke.

You came to stay one weekend when B traveled for work, a few years before you disappeared. In the morning, we walked to the park where the cherry blossoms had opened, scattering their taffy-colored petals onto the ground like tree-confetti. We went to the matinee—*Other People*, a 2016 film starring Jesse Plemons and Molly Shannon about a son suffering his mother's terminal illness. We ate popcorn, split a box of Junior Mints. We ate dinner at the restaurant down the street from my apartment and drank tea in the morning.

—Do I have that right?

We had plans for an early matinee of *Other People* downtown, but I wanted you to see the flowers before we went to the movie. I misjudged the time, how long it would take to walk to the tree where you took a series of photographs of the flowers and chose a small collection of their discarded parts from the ground to put on your altar at home.

I was annoyed: that is the missing detail.

I was annoyed by the traffic getting downtown. Why had I chosen a theater so far from my neighborhood? Why did I decide to take us all the way downtown on a Sunday?

I was annoyed—did you know that? I can't ask you anymore. I don't even remember what we talked about in the car ride there, or what you thought about the movie.

Afterwards, I couldn't stop thinking about the moment in the story where it becomes clear the mother will die. I couldn't stop thinking about that, though I never once remembered my irritation until I replayed this day in the After Time. In the After Time, I see it all differently.

I can remember the part of the movie that horrified me, but I can't remember what we talked about in the car.

Everyone gets bothered by their mothers, a friend tells me. Of course I know this. But in the aftermath, this moment's sticky residue prevents me from shaking off the guilty feeling of my annoyance about running late, when all you were doing was gathering beauty. I can't shake it from myself the way the petals had shook loose from their blossoms.

"Oh Kristin, silly girl! I don't even remember that day—what movie did we see? Let it go," you would say, flitting your hand in the air as if to swat my perseveration away like a bug before kissing my face.

You would say, "Stop punishing yourself, Kristin." You always said that, as if it would just be so easy.

One year later you called on the phone and said they found *something*.

I didn't know what missing the folding, the collected pennies and rocks would leave.

See also GHOSTS.

MIDDLE. In stories, the viewer/reader often meets the complications in the middle—the setbacks. The viewer/reader might ask what the characters are showing or withholding, or what is yet to be revealed. The middle usually foreshadows the ending, the effects on the protagonist.

The day after we brought you home from the hospital, you could no longer walk. Our family gathered. We were learning what dying at home meant. We practiced squirting morphine into Dixie cups while the hospice nurse observed. B hugged me in the hallway, worked from the kitchen at your parents' home where we kept you so he could hold my hand in the evenings. J and I took turns spooning pudding into your mouth. Everyone helped.

—Have I already mentioned the pudding?

I think I've lost the order of things, even though order is the only thing I am trying to keep; the upside-down-ness permeates everything, including my attempts at control.

Time folded in half: standing to not standing, eating to not eating, talking to not talking—each of these separated only by a single moment, not months or years as I anticipated.

In the middle, a reader might wonder, *What will happen next?*, for example. Or the reader might wonder, *What will change about this narrator? Will she find a certain kind of faith to get her through? Will she actually find a way to traverse time? Why does she keep returning to the end?*

You might be wondering these things too. You might be watching me write about you wondering these things, pondering what happens when the expected middle never materializes, when a story goes one way before it parts ways with itself, and then concludes.

See also ZETA.

MINKOWSKI SPACETIME treats time as a four-dimensional space manifold—x, y, z *and* t (time). Einstein later used this as his framework for special relativity. Minkowski spacetime is flat; particles move in straight trajectories, but Einstein's model curved them.

In Christopher Nolan's *Interstellar*, a 2014 blockbuster starring Matthew McConaughey and Jessica Chastain, the film's protagonist, NASA pilot Joseph Cooper, abandons his life as a widowed farmer and travels into another dimension to investigate its viability for human life. At the film's climax, Cooper slips into a black hole where he witnesses events spanning multiple periods of time. In the black hole, time is a physical dimension expressed as infinite lines he can observe and experience.

He can't time-travel back, but in one pivotal moment preceding the film's resolution, Cooper sees his daughter. He screams to her, though she cannot hear him.

I watch this scene on YouTube again and again now. The film violates many principles of quantum physics, but I don't watch it to understand a possibility—he's trapped, after all. He shouts, and she walks away.

I watch because there is a moment where McConaughey pivots towards the camera, where he stops screaming, and his face goes twisted in a silent anguish. I usually pause right there—as the beams of lights from the other moments of his life, the past where he looks at her through the infinite lines—refract from his space helmet into his own eyes. His own face. He stops because he accepts something right then, and I don't know what the word for that is called. It is the thing that abuts his agony, which I have not yet internalized.

But the screaming: it is the same as the missing inside me.

MIRAGE. At the UPS store, carousels stuffed full with greeting cards and corresponding envelopes turn with a creaky wheeze. A stack of various configurations of boxes rests against a wall hung with packing tape and felt markers. I hold a folder of documents: letters to credit agencies explaining the bank fraud, a check-list of phone numbers, a hospital bill you aren't here to pay.

At the front of the line, I learn the notary whose signature J and I need to close one of your accounts is on lunch break, so I stand outside, waiting in the sunshine, wondering what the Mystery Kristin Keane does on a rare morning when the summer fog has lifted off the city. I imagine her sauntering up the block past the pet store as she casually sips from a straw filled with soda—a break from the heat.

"Whatcha doin'?" she'd say, resting beside me where I lean against the storefront glass.

"What do you think?" I'd ask. I'd hold up the folder, lift my eyebrows incredulously, gesturing at the letter to Experian.

"Oh, *that* still?" she'd ask, taking a pull from her straw. "Nice day," she'd say, surveying the busy sidewalk where a delivery truck lifts crates of fresh vegetables from its backend.

"Yes, this *still*—the name theft, remember?"

She'd scrunch her face up as a cloud rolled overhead putting out the sunlight. "Right," she'd say. "—Remember when we stole the doll clothes from your neighbor?" she'd ask. "It was so easy back then."

"That wasn't *you*," I'd say, "That was *me*. We are *not* the same person."

"Your mom was so mad." She'd shake her head, smiling sentimentally. "Your problem wasn't that you broke the rules, it was that you got caught doing it."

I can remember feeling your eyes behind me as I pulled the dress over my doll's head, the sick feeling in my stomach full of breach.

"Where did you get those, Kristin?" you asked, already knowing the catalogue of my things so well—toys, like my television shows, I treated with intensive repetition.

The fistful of doll smocks and pantsuits lay in a small pile of sleeves and hems on the carpet where I sat. Planning the moment for weeks, I had stuffed them in my pocket when my friend left her room to retrieve a snack.

"—But she has so many things," I said to the floor, knowing the thing I had risked most had arrived: your disappointment.

"I'll give them back," I said. I meant sneaking them from my pocket and returning them into her hoard of things without her acknowledgement, on some other day.

"You're going to fix this," you said, before walking me to the neighbor's door and stepping back.

"Taking things is wrong—right?" Mystery Kristin Keane would ask, as if she could hear me remembering you. "My mom didn't like it, either."

Didn't like it: the past tense.

When the bell on the UPS door would ring as the notary slid through flipping the sign to "open," I'd turn back to her, but she would already be steps away.

"Good luck with that *still*," she'd call over her shoulder winking, strolling towards a patch of sunlight breaking through a cloud. *See also* FIX; X.

MIRRORS. In stories, mirrors are often used as a device for moments of contemplation and self-reflection, as well as to showcase turning points where characters experience revelations. Key scenes including mirrors in films such as *Taxi Driver, The Shining*, and *Psycho* are used to build suspense of time's passing; in others—*Alice Through the Looking-Glass* and *Poltergeist*—mirrors work as portals to other worlds. In literature, mirrors serve as symbols in works interrogating time and identity, such as Oscar Wilde's *The Picture of Dorian Grey* and the Brothers Grimm's *Snow White*.

Our new home's bathroom is mirrorless. For the first two weeks, I brush my teeth at the wall each night, pulling toothpaste from a box on the ground. I apply mascara with a small hand mirror. At Home Depot, I study the medicine cabinets, and learn the difference between recessed and wall-mounted types. I learn the difference between anchoring screws into drywall and drilling screws into studs.

My father arrives with a pencil and measuring tape. He draws a line around the cabinet while I hold it up shakily.

He asks about the other side of the wall. I explain the air gap between our home and the neighbors', a pencil-thin line separating our properties. He asks if I've met them and I say I haven't; they won't answer their door.

Hello, I had written on a note. *I am Kristin Keane. My husband and I live next door.* I left it inside their mailbox.

The next day my father returns with a saw, explaining he's been up all night worrying about the studs' location in the wall, if the cabinet would fit over the sink, if he'd be cutting through to the other side. He uses B's level. He takes a breath and makes a crude slice into the sheetrock. By the end of the morning, the hole grows to resemble a crooked picture frame, exposing the inside slats of wood from the 1950s—nails as old as you. Then he stops.

"I'm afraid to cut into the wall. I'll be back," he says, then leaves.

That night, I brush my teeth and look into the hole. I think about the other side, wondering what is there, wondering if there is another me on the other side of it, brushing her teeth, looking back. I spit into the sink. I look at that hole.

Hello, I'm Kristin Keane, I write in another note. *My husband and I are your new neighbors.* This time I put it on their doorstep.

My father brings help a few days later. They look at the hole together. They measure the studs. They cut. The hole gets covered over with a giant mirror by the afternoon.

Now, there is no more middle distance; just me looking at my own self.

That evening, in the new sets of mirrors which can be turned towards each other, I look at myself, but never really see the thing I hope for: the other version—the Before Me, unaware of how time colludes with missing, who doesn't yet know this feeling. I want to get her back.

I consider Kant's three questions. Your absence persists but does not become easier; the phone goes on blinking, but you are not on the other end of the line—that's *what I know. What I may hope* is if I look carefully enough a portal will open up in the glass of these mirrors, and I will see you waving back from another place. Is that what Kant meant? Is the question even rhetorical?

What should I do? I could ask the hundred Kristin Keanes reflected back, but I'm not sure which one of those—the one from the Before Time or the one now, blinking her eyes at all of me—is the one I need to reach for. It is unclear which of them will know how to proceed from here.

There are characters and themes and settings, but this experience is changing everything I know about how stories can go.

Would these responses satisfy Kant?

What did he do when his mother died?

See also KANT, IMMANUEL.

MOVIES. The role and importance of mothers, as well as conceptions of motherhood and the experience of becoming a mother, have been important themes explored throughout the history of cinema. In Walt Disney's 1941 animated film *Dumbo,* for example, the protagonist's mother is confined to a circus cage after defending her son from ridicule; later, the two are reunited when he becomes a media sensation.

In *Deconstructing Attachment Theory: Naturalizing the Politics of Motherhood*, feminist scholar Susan Franzblau notes that while Disney films romanticize conceptions of femininity, female heroines are typically motherless because their mothers are either absent, dead, or evil (see *Pinocchio, Peter Pan, The Sword in the Stone, The Little Mermaid, Beauty and the Beast, Aladdin, Bambi, The Fox and The Hound, The Hunchback of Notre Dame,* and *Tarzan*).

In 1938, Walt Disney's mother Flora died by accidental asphyxiation at the age of 70. She had complained for several days about a gas leak in the new home her sons purchased for her in the Hollywood neighborhood of Los Angeles. Many speculate Walt Disney felt responsible, though many of his works featured motherless children even before her death.

We loved to go to the movies together. When you worked extra jobs on weekends cleaning houses in the '80s and '90s, I'd join you first in the Oakland Hills, wiping down wooden stair banisters, scrubbing the insides of toilet bowls with Comet and long plastic brushes. Sometimes you gave me a section of floor to vacuum, a table, or a patch of linoleum to polish with cleaner.

"Here, Kristin," you'd say, pointing into a dark bathroom before turning on the lights and illuminating a long double vanity stacked with mirrored trays of glass perfume bottles, gold compacts of cosmetics. Fancy bathrooms with carpeted flooring.

"Remember?" you'd ask, demonstrating how to hold the Formula 409 six inches from the dusting rag, its spray cascading a foamy stream onto the fibers. "In circles like this. And lift *up* the things—don't just dust around them."

You usually went back over my work with careful precision after I'd become distracted by the leaves outside windows I had wiped clean, or got lost running my hands along the stretches of bookcases and entire rooms dedicated to children's play: board games and air hockey tables, small trampolines and boxes filled with the sets of Legos I wanted most. I spent a lot of my time then envious of things other children had.

Still: you showed me how to be quiet in someone else's universe. How to move with careful work, righting corners, fluffing things, pulling folds into neat, orderly angles. How to notice things. How to keep going. How to work with grace.

Afterwards—or the next morning—our reward were those matinees. In Disney animations, the mothers' death always unsettled me; a world without you in it felt unfathomable.

But they buttressed my love for story: I was learning about how neat resolutions could be formed, even if they bumped against our own reality. There wasn't money for the food dehydrator, there was want for solutions, for easements always.

In the dark, we shared licorice sticks. We watched the story always conclude as it should: the desire and need satisfied, the problem overcome.

NEWTON, SIR ISAAC (1642-1727) was one of the world's most influential thinkers, perhaps most famous for formulating the laws of motion. Albert Einstein's theories of relativity were based on Newton's ideas: a body at rest remains at rest; acceleration by force is related to magnitude of force and the mass of the object; for every action there is an equal and opposite reaction. Newton's laws have held stable, but other laws have been developed over time. Those we didn't yet know functioned—though of course they did—even before discovery.

My father came to see you before you disappeared.

"Hello, dear," he said. I had never heard him name you in endearment. He kissed you on the forehead, the hand. He held your hand.

"There are tigers in the persimmon trees," you said. There was a change in the way you breathed and then we were holding your hands. We bathed your arms with wet washcloths. We murmured into your ears all the things you meant to us. We read you *Goodnight Moon* and taped photographs to the walls. We lay beside you and cradled your head.

Then there was no language left—just the tear that slipped from your eye and ran down your face.

I don't remember my father ever kissing your hand—I can't even recall memories of a time when we lived in the same place—the same house where I found the finch in the street. But I will always remember how he kissed your forehead that last day.

In the end, nothing happened as expected.

J. William Worden's four tasks of mourning outline grieving as accepting the reality of the loss, experiencing grief pain, adjusting to the new environment, and finding connection while moving forward after the loss of a loved one. But really, these models cannot be affixed to every mourner's experience: there is pain afterwards, and then there is living with it—an enterprise as unique as fingerprints.

I'm saying we can get very attached to the ways in which we believe things happen—to the rules, laws, and math equations that govern them. What we fail so often to realize—to remember—is even the most promising ideas can eventually be turned on their heads.

See also EINSTEIN, ALBERT; TIDES.

NONEXISTENT OBJECTS make up a theoretical class of objects philosophers have explored—such as the fountain of youth, the square circle, or the unicorn—that do not actually exist in any material way, yet have clear qualities. Some embrace the concept, while others find it illogical.

On a trip to Los Angeles in the fall, I jog on Figueroa Street. A man looks at himself where two strips of mirror come together at an ATM. I run past, my hips flashing across them in reflection. He pulls his lips back to investigate his gums as if to say, *What is this inside of me?* As if to say, *What even is me anymore?*

You can reflect yourself, I want to tell him.

You can ask 'What should I do?' I want to tell him, *though there will probably be no response. You can even imagine things.*

I keep hoping to pull the medicine cabinet doors apart when I do this at home, and see you standing behind me in the bathroom of our '90s apartment. It will be any morning we shared again—I'm not picky. I will brush my teeth while you fuss with your curling iron, its wire twisted and pulled across the sink. J will be there, too, applying a perfect line of eyeshadow. We won't say much to one another because we won't realize we should, though there may be a discussion of logistics.

"Are you working tonight?" you might ask me.

"Yes," I might say.

"I'll come see you for dinner, then?"

I'll nod. Dinner means a stroll through J.C. Penny's, Taco Bell and The Candy Stop for watermelon rings. It means you in the stationers with the music boxes finding your favorite one, "Memories," which you'll play while I stand waiting, before you walk me back to my shift where I will go on selling wallets and ties.

It will just be any day.

It is so easy to do this, I want to tell the man at the ATM. *It is so easy to slip into the place you want to be, without ever even leaving the dimension you're in.*

What is the math for that?

See also GESTALT EMPTY CHAIR.

NOVIKOV SELF-CONSISTENCY PRINCIPLE states that in time travel, if an event exists which would produce a change in the past, the probability of that event in a universe with one timeline equals zero—in effect making time paradoxes impossible. Meaning, those able to travel back would have to act consistently parallel to what had already taken place, unlike the way characters so often behave in time-travel narratives.

Yet the premise of *Quantum Leap* trained us entirely on the presumption that history *can* be changed. In episode forty-four Sam travels back to 1957 to prevent Moe Stein—the star of a children's show, *Captain Galaxy*—from dying. Moe has invented the Time-Onometer, a time machine he hopes will repair his damaged relationship with his daughter. But Sam realizes that Moe shares his theory: time works like a string which can be tied into a loop and bundled up to enable movement back and forth within one's life.

"And then each day of your life would touch another day," Sam says to Moe. "And then, you could travel from one place on the string to another, thus enabling you to move back and forth within your own lifetime—*maybe*."

"That's it… That's it," Moe says. "Then I could actually…"

"Quantum leap?" Sam asks.

Moe smiles.

In the climax, Moe detonates the Time-Onometer, spoiling his own plans, but his daughter Irene—freshly made aware of his hopes to fix the past—assures him there's still plenty of time left for them to be a family. He gives her the flowers he intended to bring back to his dead wife.

Sam manages to protect Moe, help him repair his relationship with his daughter, *and* confirm his own theory all in one episode—in the end, always putting right what once went wrong.

Why did we love these episodes so much—a storyline with such a clearly faulty premise? Sam got propelled into so many preposterous premises, yet we always cheered him on. There was hope in that, I suppose, in believing time could be wrangled somehow. It is a resistance to the math equations, the realities of the universe.

Revisiting the episodes is a vehicle. It is also a way to turn away from the missing, to drop myself into an imaginative plane where anything is possible.

See also FOURTH DIMENSION.

OCTOPUSES are mollusks that typically live in tropical waters, though they can be found in all of Earth's oceans—species live on ocean floors and coral reefs, and some are pelagic, occupying open waters somewhat proximal to the surface. They have a beak, two eyes, eight limbs, and a large mantel at the back of the head containing organs. Some species have a sac which releases ink to aid in escaping from danger. Known for their ability to shift shape to get into or out of unusually confined and tight locations, octopuses' soft tissues are able to bend, twist, be held rigid, and camouflage into various surroundings. They are solitary and typically live for one to two years, surviving on other ocean life such as lobster and shrimp.

Curious if animals could recognize themselves in mirrors, psychologist Gordon G. Gallup began experimenting with chimpanzees at what would later be called the Tulane National Primate Research Center. Initially the chimps treated their own reflection as if it were one of its kind, displaying aggression and sexual gestures. In time, though, they realized they were looking at themselves, and soon used the mirrors to inspect their mouths and nether regions.

Researchers began testing the mirrors with other animals—great apes, elephants, and dolphins, who all expressed the self-awareness and intellectual capacity required to recognize oneself according to a mirror test. They noticed that the body projected back looked like their own, and when anaesthetized and marked, acknowledged the markings on themselves.

Octopuses do not pass this test.

—

The octopuses made us not ourselves anymore—not a mother and daughter, but two creatures surrounded by sea monsters which were no longer outside the frame of the image of you at the sea, but inside it now, everywhere.

Almost exactly a year after your diagnosis, your scan returned clear. The doctors were cautious. They took you off of medications—insurance wouldn't cover them without evidence of cancer. I worried about the optimism you held. Each visit had become a vortex to the next—an endless chain of worrying about the outcome, the next bit of news. I worried about my worrying. *You* worried about my worrying.

The spring came. You made citronella candles to ward off mosquitos. You flew back and forth to Sedona to see friends, put a small pool up in the sunshine for my nieces to splash inside. For months, my octopus stayed at bay, pinned against my insides where it waited.

We went on. A body scan was scheduled for fall and my stomach knotted when I considered it. I traveled to New Labrador in the summer, reaching out each day with a text or call. *How are you?* I'd ask or write nervously. Then, a relief-wave came by way of your emoji responses: a kissy face, a rainbow; I could relax until the next input of information.

Fall arrived. You cancelled the scan I had dreaded for months. My father's sister had passed, and the funeral was set for that same day. She was home watering the lawn in her bare feet before I left that summer, then soon after I came back, she couldn't walk.

She was here, then she was gone.

"I'll reschedule for later," you said, but by then there were three nodules in your lungs, small beans of melanoma. They had options for us, though. They always had options.

In the elevator leaving the hospital, you asked: "What does stage four mean?"

"It means something not good," I said to the buttons.

My octopus kicked up. Why did we wait almost two extra months for results? Looking back, those two months could have been the trigger point. They might have bought more medication, more intervention, more *time.*

It extended into my arms, my legs. It came undone. I looked at the elevator buttons.

"Metastasis" means change. I could have said that. I could have offered to hug you. I could have lied to you, said everything would be just fine. But I could only think about the arrow, about a time I didn't know—only that inside of it, things would not be the same. I had lost control to its myth—there was only forward direction you would not be here for.

I think about that scene in the elevator all the time. That scene was a turning point of the story that is inside of figuring out the story now.

What is that part of a narrative called?

See also FRACTURE.

OTHER SIDE. It is typical, when you've experienced a difficulty, for people to say things like, *You're going to get on the other side of this, just wait. Just give it time.* People say this even if they don't know what that side really feels like.

After you disappeared, others said *you* had gone to the other side. As if they understood that the other side is somehow preferable. As if it's not better for you to be here with me and J, with our family. It is better there, whatever *there* is. It is better there, *however* there was.

Newton believed that space had a dimension, but he did not think the objects inside it could affect that space. Einstein believed they could.

"Forgive me, Newton," he wrote, in dissent.

Then he added time as a fourth dimension to space's width, height and length. This gives promise, this alternative. Einstein's teacher Minkowski gave us spacetime, but Einstein curved it: a bend in the rules.

Perhaps I am just cherry-picking here now, trying to make things fit together that don't, but with each new fact I gather, I am able to shuffle them inside these entries as if I am filing clues. In this part of the story—where the protagonist attempts to get closer to a kind of truth, to solve the puzzle—you would usually begin vocalizing your concern.

"What's going to happen?" you would ask the televlsion screen at every turning point before looking to me.

Now you might say with worry, "What will happen to you, Kristin, my love?".

I have spent a lot of time thinking about this other side and what you might like it to be. Supposedly, this other side is better. Paradise could be filled with your favorite things: seashells, bird feathers, flowers. It could be everything you've ever wanted. But maybe you are trapped screaming through a window I can't hear you from, while on my side I search, like Sam Cooper in *Interstellar*. We could both be screaming, turning away in anguish.

What if it's you watching me writing about you screaming? Watching me writing about *Interstellar*?

"Oh Kristin, that's so dark!" you would say. "What if the other side is a side that another part of you is here with me now, that you just don't know or feel yet? What if we *are* together right now and just don't understand it?"

You see what I'm doing—don't you? I am trying to give you a voice that you no longer have.

The other side is better for the both of us, they say. But if the side I am going to get to eventually through supposed healing, and the side you are on, are not in fact the same, and they are both the other side of here, then how can that be?

How can that be.

I am not getting any better and we are nearing the end of the alphabet.

See also MIDDLE.

OUT OF THIS WORLD. Running four seasons from 1987-1991, the plot of NBC's *Out of This World* centers on Evie Garland, who learns at thirteen that her father is an extraterrestrial. Voiced by the actor Burt Reynolds, Troy Garland is never fully visible to the audience, but he communicates regularly with Evie from outer space, through a device called "The Cube." Evie can keep time suspended, alter events, and transport herself.

As a child, I loved the idea of the cube, how its lights pulsated and flashed, how Evie could relieve herself of any kind of jam. Of course I understood she could stop time—but my focus wasn't on the gift of that, but the reaction of the cast: would the other actors *actually* hold themselves as stiffly as necessary to represent a kind of freeze? Never once did I consider the magnitude of what that kind of power could mean for loss, how the cube opened on a hinge like a mouth, speaking for someone out of sight.

I imagine asking the Mystery Kristin Keane how she endures not being able to stop time from going on.

"Oh, you're still in that phase?" she'd ask.

I'd look at my hands for a moment. "Well, I *know* that she—,"

"It's okay," she'd interrupt. "You don't have to explain. I understand what you're doing … Is that her?"

She'd point to the photograph of you inside the altar box.

"She's very pretty," she'd say as she fingered the dried flowers, the seashells I've left on its ledge. "So much light."

"How do you communicate?" I'd ask, thinking of how Evie would nestle into the covers on her bed or her window seat, speaking so naturally with the person not really there in the frame.

She'd take a photo from the box—the film strip of the two of us. "Oh, the missing," she'd say to herself before putting it back.

"The missing? Is that really your response to that question?" I'd ask.

"Yes," she'd say. "That is my answer to every one of your questions."

When I watch episodes over now, I fast forward to Evie in the window with the stars in the sky. Before I thought it was star-gazing, imagining her father in space, but now I understand what we are supposed to pay attention to in these scenes: her yearning eyes.

PLUTARCH (46-120 CE). A Greek philosopher and prolific writer, Plutarch was the author of works largely concerned with ethics and philosophical questions touching on far-ranging topics such as art, psychology, and theology.

The author of at least two-hundred twenty-seven texts, he is most famous for *Parallel Lives,* a collection of paired biographies comparing the characters of significant Greek and Roman soldiers and statesmen, which form a sort of moral instruction composed through their life stories, struggles, and accomplishments. The reader, he believed, would become inspired to embody the characters of the historical figures.

Parallel Lives is about the moral struggle of good and bad, being alive and having a destiny. Plutarch believed in reincarnation and a separation of the soul from the body in death. When his two-year-old daughter died, he pled with his wife not to grieve her, reminding her of all her blessings. "Only, my dear wife," he wrote, "in your emotion keep me as well as yourself within bounds." He begged her to put her sorrow aside, to not give into grief's great manipulations—how it lies beside you, how it slicks itself onto your skin. "… once it has fixed itself with the passing of time and become his companion and household intimate, it will not quit him even at his earnest desire."

Plutarch instructed his wife to control her emotions, but he also wanted to know if a ship with entirely replaced parts would remain the same ship. The discourse surrounding this thought experiment often centers on drawing lines and boundaries around what constitutes embodiment. Is it still the same ship with a replaced bow? Is it still the same ship with a replaced sail? Is it still the same ship if every single part of the boat is replaced but one single plank or nail?

Until finally: is it still *it* once the last nail is succeeded?

But I wonder, really, if this is a puzzle of philosophy, or actually an inquiry of grief.

I know now one doesn't really understand the meaning of Plutarch's question until a thing that is loved disappears.

I'm saying I don't believe Plutarch was only writing to his wife; I believe he was also writing to himself.

The ship is the daughter and the grief the parts of the boat he hopes to understand in its dismantling.

—Or maybe the boat is him.

—Or maybe the boat is me—each part of myself changing with the missing, perhaps evolving into another kind of love. Perhaps with you gone, reshaped into another person entirely.

Barthes wrote, "I do not strive to put my present expression in the service of my previous truth (in the classical system, such an effort would have been sanctified under the name of *authenticity*), I abandon the exhausting pursuit of an old piece of myself, I do not try to *restore* myself (as we say of a monument). I do not say: "I am going to describe myself" but: "I am writing a text, and I call it R.B." Am I still the same person I was before, if you are gone and my identity has been taken? What really am I anymore, if not your daughter, if not the name you gave me?

"I myself am my own symbol," Barthes writes. "I am the story which happens to me …" Sooner than later, I will need to find my way out of this.

See also: SOUL.

POPEIL, RONALD (1935-CURRENT). Ronco, a manufacturing company founded in 1964 by Ron Popeil, produces goods including the inside-the-egg Egg Scrambler, Pocket Fisherman, Smokeless Ashtray, and the Popeil Automatic Pasta Maker. A family-trained kitchen gadget salesman, Popeil became a marketing pioneer promoting Ronco's line of inexpensive inventions through innovative marketing campaigns.

In those hours between morning soap operas and gameshows, and afternoon sitcoms and talk shows, the Ronco Electric Food Dehydrator informercial was a familiar, dependable landscape. Shiny bags of dried fruits—shrunken strawberries, wheels of pineapple, wedges of apples, plump and juicy raisins—reclined in cellophane bags in a makeshift kitchen.

Then, it appeared he spoke directly to me, offering *me* a very special price. In two easy payments, it could be mine.

He snapped an onion across the mandolin, stressing its uniform slices, promising only tears of joy.

"Hello," I say. I look at my hands. The fog is in the yard.

"Hello," I say.

I keep imagining the Panasonic, the mustard shag carpet, Ron Popeil in the background peddling his goods. There are the dragonflies pinned into shadow boxes inside the curio cabinet, the furniture's legs wedged deeply into the pile of shag carpeting beside the television.

I try imagining you.

"Hello," I say.

I try to imagine myself describing the persimmon harvest to you—their pulpy insides, the boxes of fruit I picked for my students this season. I imagine telling you about how heavy the trees hung with fruit, about how the trees make me cry when they bow down in the orchard, how all I can think about is you standing between them, beside the place where I married B, blowing me a kiss. I try imagining you. I imagine telling you that Ron Popeil is still alive, that this fall, after you disappeared, I finally bought a dehydrator just like I always dreamed. I sliced the persimmons into thin rings and placed them into the trays and turned the machine on, and when the machine withered them down, they did not look like persimmons anymore but they looked a lot like the hummingbird's eyes even though they were the color of marmalade, even though I put them into my mouth, even though I sliced into my finger with the knife while I was cutting them apart. I was thinking about you while I took them one by one—the fruit I picked from the trees in your parents' orchard—to cut apart, to dry, to make them in a way, to try at least, to make them into a kind of forever.

"What was the light like between the trees?" you would ask me and I'd wonder if you could remember what that fruit meant to our family, how it was a kind of our love.

"It gleamed," I'd say. "It was beautiful. Just like it always is that time of year."

See also TAXIDERMY.

QUANTUM LEAP. In the final episode of the series, Sam Beckett leaps to a coal mining town. He looks into the mirror as he always does, in this case above a saloon's bar top—except this time, the face looking back is finally his own.

"Something wrong?" the bartender asks.

"That's ah, me … in the mirror," Sam says.

He touches his face, watches his own reflection, stunned.

"You let too much time go by," the bartender says, "you could lose touch with reality."

Do you remember the final episode? Sam meets various characters he's crossed paths with before, but they won't acknowledge him. He learns that day is the day of his birth—his arrival at the bar the exact *time* of his birth. As a series of confusing interactions unfolds, he realizes near the conclusion that something is still left for him to put right: he must leap in time to convey a message to Al's wife that Al is still alive, and help ensure she'll wait for him.

The viewer learns, before the credits, in a series of captions after the last scene, that Sam saves Al's marriage, and that Sam never returns home, back to where he started before the leaping began. As viewers, we're asked to consider whether it was the moment in the mirror with the bartender, Sam's disorientation with his own self, or another scene obscured in darkness before the captions reveal his choice—that he decides, finally, to give himself up to the throes of time and always keep leaping.

This surprise ending, in the show's last possible moment, is a pivot from Sam's constant objective throughout the series. What if we had looked away when we watched the finale together? What if we had turned the television off right as the last scene closed? We would have thought that, in the end, Sam got what he'd always wanted: to go home.

Stories are designed for us to read or watch, but we make choices about how far we want to see them through.

"My leap had taken a quantum twist," Sam says in voice-over as he pieces together the upside-down-ness of the final episode, the strange circumstances of characters he recognizes who say they've never met him. "I no longer knew what was real and what was imagined—and if imagined, whose mind was imagining it. Mine—or someone else's."

Let's say this entry is a denouement. You can end your reading here, if you'd like. It will be better on your heart, whatever or wherever that is anymore. Let's say, like in those final moments of *Quantum Leap*, that I get to go home, in a way.

I can tell you, here, in this entry, that I am okay. The days begin and end, and I am able to smile and laugh now. I haven't fallen into the sea. The math, the physics principles, are too complex, though I puzzle them constantly when running, sitting in traffic with your photo still in the jockey box of my car. Scientists and mathematicians say equations are discovered in the same way I might stumble upon a rolled-up dollar in a coat pocket. This is a reductive comparison, I know, but we hold onto such ideas as if they are the only truths. Wolfgang Pauli, a pioneer of quantum physics, wrote to colleagues in 1930 after making an unlikely discovery, "I have done a terrible thing, I have postulated a particle that cannot be detected." Some of this science is based on faith, but I accept it, too.

Let's say I build more altars for you, that I have accepted that you are gone. That is a kind of going home, is it not?

If you do decide to keep reading, you should ask yourself about resolutions, about the kind of story you are willing to accept.

See also TWISTS.

QUANTUM MECHANICS involves the interactions of sub-atomic particles—those smaller than an atom—and their motion throughout the universe. MRI machines' technology (you sat in many) is made possible by quantum physics. We clung to those machines' outputs, we held on to each other's hands in the oncology room, waiting for images the machine produced: nebulous shapes I forced to represent the soft edges of roses, peonies. The rounded forms of your grandmother's hydrangeas. We waited for images to tell us what to worry about next.

Just days before we left for Mexico, I read that researchers at Yale University detected the quantum leaps of an artificial atom as it shifted from a "bright" to "dark" state, settling decades-long debates about leaping atoms Einstein insisted were just expressions of randomness. They *can* be controlled, these things. These leaps. It's a small step on an extremely small scale, but now I cling to the possibility of controlling these jumps, the way I clung to the images in the doctors' offices that I pretended were blossoming flowers. I imagined them telling us that everything growing inside you was light. That everything growing inside you was good, as beautiful as you. Each a petal on a stem, pulsing with life.

RAFT. On a trip to the Grand Canyon just before B and I married, my raft flipped in a rapid. I never told you that. I never told you how I asked, before we hit the wave train, exactly what we were supposed to do if it appeared we would roll. You would call this a premonition. You would say I had intuited it. I only know that I saw the wave and how it licked the sky. I saw its tentacles' shape.

My foot slipped from the hold and I was under. It was the loudest thing I ever heard, louder than sirens. It pulsed. I never told you that—how scared I was falling off that raft, losing my grip, tumbling under the water the way I might if I fell from the sky. You would have been too frightened.

My memory still holds the familiarity of the current—and that was years ago—but sometimes now it is very hard to remember the exact color blue of your eyes.

RECOGNIZE. From "re" (again) and "cognoscere," (to learn).

I have to make some meaning from this. I consider what you look like now, if you are on another side, and whether you will understand me. Will you still know my freckles, the way I laugh? I realize my questions have begun repeating themselves, but it is because I still cannot wrap my mind around this: you are stuck to everything all the time, and you are not even visible.

This is a very painful labor, this missing—so much more difficult than I ever could have imagined it would be. You will hate hearing that, but it is the truth.

In Hawaii, while you sat on the shore, I snorkeled nearby. A series of photographs you took from a beach towel on the rock traces me from the shore into the water, until I'm just a tube poking from it. Under there were the turtles you couldn't see but wanted to. I met their silver-dollar-sized eyes as their bodies rocked in the current, ribbons of kelp shifting between us. Under there was quiet; I heard my own breath.

You were always looking for me.

I don't know what that's like—to want to look so hard at a thing you've made.

As my face changes and wrinkles at the eyes, my hair will gray, and I'll change in ways I'm not sure you will recognize.

Yes, maybe this is what I fear most: that I really don't believe I'll ever be with you again. That I don't know what the resolution will be.

RESIDUE is related to the computational world, like 'residuum;' the remainder. The number left over when one number is divided by another. Residue also refers to substances found after processes like combustion, evaporation—things that naturally remain, like ashes, like a soggy deck after the fog. Like the feeling of sorrow when your mother dies.

Residue persists, it resides, it remains. Sometimes you have no choice but to get used to it.

The Mystery Kristin Keane sticks to everything, too. She reminds me of the potential versions of myself on the horizon line. The Before Me versus the After Me.

Loan-Confidant writes.

Hello, Kristin, they say. They tell me again they've escalated my issue to their collections department.

I ask for confirmation. I ask for help.

Thank you for your patience, they say. They tell me where I can follow up with
   information on my missed payments. They will get back to me as soon as possible.
   See also AFTERLIFE; ALPHABET.

RETURNS can refer to profits on investments, results in an election, or the act of putting something back. "Return" is also a key that commands the return of a carriage on a standard typewriter, or the corresponding end of a line in a word processor. Return means to go back, send back, come back.
   Return. In this other ending, it is worth considering the quality of a word which consumes me now:

Returns Regarding Resurrections
A resurrection is a return to life from death—a concept present in the central writings and doctrines of several world religions. In Greek mythology, many figures are brought into immortality through a death-event. For many religions, a kind of paradise—the place where a god or gods reside—is where good followers go to live eternally, yet they are not brought back to life necessarily. They are, themselves, enhanced.

Returns Regarding the Things I Cling To
I returned to your apartment once, before we packed up your things. I sat on your bed. I tried to put myself where you used to lie. I tried putting my body in the same place where you slept. I put my face in your clothes. I opened your medicine cabinet door. I read the notes affixed to the interior in scotch tape. I tried memorizing the words. I tried putting the shape of each of your letters to memory. I put water in your tea kettle. I drank tea from your coffee cup. I tried to hold the cup like you held it. I stood at the altar on your dresser. I touched each energy card with the tips of my fingers. I closed my eyes the way you did when you chose them. I tried feeling their power like you showed me. I touched your sage, a bird feather, a small glass vial filled with sand and animal teeth. I sat in your car. I put my hands on the steering wheel. I tried situating them in the exact place you put your hands. I opened your trunk. I imagined I was you opening the trunk. I touched each thing inside: a blanket, a spare tire. I tried remembering their

form exactly. I touched your wind chimes. I closed my eyes. I let my hair blow in my face. I tried feeling the way you might have felt with the sun on your mouth. I put my hands up like you did in the wind. I put my face into a sunflower you grew on your patio. I returned to your apartment just beside the persimmon orchard. I went back to the bathroom. I opened your medicine cabinet door. I read the notes affixed to the interior in scotch tape: they were about tomorrow, they were about loving yourself. I tried memorizing the words. I tried.

Return Questions
If the deceased's concept of paradise is to continue living in their current life, why are they not visible to those they've left behind? If the deceased stated that in death, she "would be everywhere," why is she not yet visible to those she's left behind? If the deceased left a collection of small taxidermized animals in her closet, why is the hummingbird who died long before she disappeared still visible in the closet, but the deceased is not?

Returns Regarding Responses
Loan-Confidant writes back. They tell me again they have escalated my issue and will get back to me as soon as possible.

They thank me in advance for my patience.

SEA. I can hardly bear to look at my favorite picture of you anymore because it is everything I miss: you at the sea. The photograph is about losing the light inside it, but it is also about the waves churning at your feet. There was no knowing then that the beach my father photographed you on before you ever put me in the universe would become the beach I now live beside. I walk on it now, each week. I put my feet in the same spot and turn away from the sun.

When I'm there, I look at the sand, the water, I contort my body into the same shape you have in the photograph, I crouch towards the tide. I bend myself to look at the sea. I smile.

No—I don't smile. I can't smile. I *imagine* myself smiling.

Plutarch wants to know if a ship with entirely replaced parts is in fact the same ship. I want to know if I can ever really stand on the sand in the same place you once stood forty-seven years ago. That is the thing about the sea: *can* it be the same, if the specks of sand and drops of water have changed?

That is the matter, really, I think. It is about changing and continuing to change without you—the After Me smiling again, but never in the same way as Before.

See also MANY-WORLDS INTERPRETATION; WAVES.

SINGAPORE is a city-state in South-East Asia and a travel destination for millions of people each year. Known as one of the largest commercial centers in the world, popular sites include the Singapore Zoo, the Marina Bay Sands and the Orchard Road district.

Four months after you disappeared, I follow B there to a conference.

This will be good for you, a friend says. The seventeen-hour flight is disorienting, but I slip easily into the upside-down-ness of traveling across the globe; its foggy rhythms are like now *is*: an axis-tilt. There, I meet contrasting slashes of neon against buildings, orchids the size of dinner plates, a humidity that reinvents the shape of my hair. I peel my clothes from my sweated skin each night in the hotel room and every corner crackles with beauty and lights.

But even eight-thousand miles from home, trapdoors fall open everywhere: malls, flowers, even colors. I dream about you almost every night when the jet lag slams down: you on a plane, in a taxi, at the end of my bed. It is always the same—you are back but you are dying again, and I cannot get to you in time.

While B works, I walk. In black and white in the tiny televisions mounted into the corners of streetlights, restaurants, coffee shops, I see myself, watching myself. On a busy sidewalk, people slide past me, as if I were a rock in a stream. They all move quickly while I stand fastened, unsure where next to go.

When I return home there are calls from a new creditor, an overdue credit card account in my name. I call. I explain I do not have this credit card. They cannot help, they say, they can only speak to Kristin Keane.

I am Kristin Keane, I say. *The real one.*

They cannot divulge the details of the account, they tell me. They cannot talk to me anymore.

See also MIRRORS.

SORROW. The days go on. They feel like Sam's string tied in the loop, pressing against each other, except all the days now are since you're gone, and they all feel exactly the same—liminal. I find heartache at the bottom of a jar of jam you gave me last winter. I don't throw it away and instead set it beside the altar where I keep flowers for you, with your crystals. I place the stem of a dried rose inside, but it is hard for me to look—you, literally in a box with your hands in the air. You are paper now, a wooden artifact.

I wash dishes at the window. I sit at the sliding glass door. B has set a ring of peonies in a vase: your and my favorite flower. I think of you. I think of those encyclopedias, how they were bound in such durable material.

There is no birdbath, no sundial.

"How do you handle the sorrow?" I'd ask the Mystery Kristin Keane.

She'd look through the window out at the wet deck.

"It sticks to everything like a glue, doesn't it?" she'd ask. "I despise it, that thing in your throat."

"Yes, I know—but how do you *handle* it?"

"You have to comfort yourself," she'd say, after a long period of considering the birds in the bushes outside. "Sometimes you have to just pretend. You have to find your own way."

"Yes, of course I already knew that. I knew that *before*."

"Not *really*, Kristin. You didn't really *know* that before."

SOUL is the immortal aspect of a person, separate from their physical shape. Some consider it the energy that lives on even when the person does not.

If a soul is immaterial, separate from the brain, I wonder whether it can change after death. How does something immaterial and unconfined to a body both have and not have boundaries? It can shift, yet goes on without a container, somehow feeling and conscious and memory-making all at once.

Or *does* it still make memories? *Are* you still making memories?

If I can change a part of my spirit into a better me, then does refashioning ever stop? Do I have a limit on how much I can shift time's shape? Part of me still wants desperately to believe I can put my hands on it.

I'm trying to tell a story about time: it is unknowable; it is beyond our grasp; it is a thing we have invented. "Time" is an idea, and yet, and *yet*—it is all we have. It is everything we know and don't know at once.

In Proto-Germanic, "saiwalo" means soul, which may be related to "saiwaz," a likely word for sea. Some speakers of Proto-Germanic believed that the final resting place for souls was at the bottom of a rock bed. The words are different, but they are almost the same, roped together as tightly as kelp is to foam, as tightly as darkness is to the resilient skins of the creatures navigating through it—lanternfish and tube worms and octopuses.

See also SEA.

TAROT refers to the practice of divination using a deck of cards designed for game play. The original deck had four suits with fourteen cards each: numbers one through ten, and a queen, king, knight, and jack. The deck also includes a fifth trump suit of twenty-one cards and a fool, forming a "major arcana" used to incite reflection into the past, present, and future. It can be used personally, or by way of an expert.

At a tarot consultation J and I took you to in the spring before you disappeared, the reader told us to ask what we wanted to be revealed and expressed in our lives. She told us to pull a card with the hand closest to our hearts: you pulled the hermit with his egg and wheat heading into darkness with a lantern above his head—then you nodded vigorously.

"Yes," you said to the reader. "I am the hermit."

A car alarm sounded in the parking lot as we sat quietly in a circle of dried sunflower, crystals and eagle feathers. Each stranger took a turn before it was mine.

I examined the possibilities and then reached, flipping over the death card. All the women in the circle gasped. J and I looked at each other. We swallowed.

"Death is your ally—this is *good*," the reader told me, quelling the crowd. "It's about killing a conditional reality." On the card, she pointed to small illustrations: fish (rebirth), snake (shedding), sea onion (death of each layer). She looked at me. She patted my hand.

Animals. The sea. Transubstantiation. Killing a part of myself which is most afraid of what time means.

See also ALPHABET.

TAXIDERMY. Preserving the skins and hides of animals is a practice humans have used for centuries, but the art of displaying entire dead animals emerged during the Enlightenment. This process involves positioning animals in life-like forms for observational study.

During my first year of college, you became an amateur taxidermist. When I returned home for the holiday season, a single maple-colored raptor laid belly and beak up toward where the sky would have been had it not found itself on a garage workbench, its dead body rescued from the side of the road. Its parts rested casually on torn-up strips of paper towels, yellowed like giant Band-Aids by the fluids leaking from its appendages. I gasped, put my hand to my mouth. I was only looking for a screwdriver.

The head and carapace were intact and waited in repose; the raptor's penny-colored eyes set into sockets, sunk back in its head. This part laid on the folded-up beach towel stamped with an image of a sunset. I tanned on that same towel beside our apartment complex pool before you moved across the valley to your parents' persimmon orchard; that was only five months before, but the dead bird was positioned on it exactly as I had once been. Its two yellow feet, drying on one of the strips, were shriveled into small, leathery curls. On another, a single wing lay by itself on the corner of the table, its rust-feathered mate still attached to the body where it belonged, the only natural thing about the entire arrangement. Three pairs of rubber-handled pliers were ordered and arranged neatly by size at the center of the table.

Taxidermy is the arrangement of skin. It is an attempt to freeze a moment of time, permanently—in gesture, even. We have inherited all these things from you, the dead in their shadow boxes, on small squares of paper towels.

What were you saying about time and the body with the dead bird you found? I so desperately wish I would have asked.

You took your last breath in the evening and I kissed your eyelids. We lay with you. Then they took you away and we waved goodbye from the porch, as we always do when someone leaves the house.

See also INSPECT; POPEIL, RONALD.

TIDES are created by gravitational forces that correspond with the moon, sun and Earth's positions and rotation. They create the rise and fall of sea levels known as low and high tide. Semi-diurnal tides cycle from high to low twice daily; diurnal tides occur just once. Sea level also fluctuates because of environmental forces, but tides are responsible for most of the short-term movement, and take place wherever a gravitational field varies in time and space.

The Bay of Fundy boasts the highest tide in the world between Nova Scotia and New Brunswick, where the difference between high and low markings can be as long as the stretch of a three-story building. Some tides are so powerful, like those in the Qiantang River in China, that during particular moon phases the surge of the tide raises a tidal bore—an upriver wave of water—as much as nine meters high.

I keep going back to the end. When will I remember clearly something different from our last moments together? These memories come in surges: when I walk to the grocery store; when I run in the park. *Today I need to...* I'll think, making a small list before a shaft of light arrives on the trail a few steps ahead, and then suddenly you are there, rising against the sand of my memory before falling away again—our hands together, then kissing your eyelids.

TOTAL RECALL. This 1990 film Starring Arnold Schwarzenegger and Sharon Stone depicts a construction worker (Schwarzenegger's Douglas Quaid) who longs to visit Mars. But when a trip to "Rekall"—a company which implants manufactured vacation memories in clients—goes wrong, Quaid gets confronted with the possibility that his entire life is a false memory. In a series of ruses, Quaid is made to believe he embodies a false identity, that he is both himself and not himself. By the final scene, though he has supposedly saved the entire population of the newly colonized Mars, he is still unsure if it's a dream. *Total Recall* was like all the other movies in the curio cabinet worn well by repetition—J and I often paused and rewound the scene where Quaid unzips himself from inside his disguise.

Adjacent to our new home is a park. For the first three days, our windows went uncovered. Steady streams of cars parked directly in front of the driveway, hazard lights winking into fog while families waited for their children. When the streetlight came on and the gate to the park closed, sometimes the cars still waited. Their lights blinked. I could not see *who* waited.

I received an email, on the third day, concerning a writing project about shared identities.

"It's just a coincidence," B said.

"Is it?" I asked, after explaining it seemed odd all this looking, all this identity-splitting taking place around me.

The next day I fixed a rod above each window frame. I slipped a curtain panel on either side. They collected on the ground. I wanted someone in one of the cars to be *you*, but I also wanted the looking to stop.

In one *Total Recall* scene, Quaid sees himself as a hologram, then inside a video.

"You're not you," he says to himself. "You're *me*."

"What do you want, Mr. Quaid?" the operatives ask him, after the narrative has twisted around so many times that even the viewer can't be sure what version of himself tells the story.

He says he wants to remember, because it will let him be himself again.

They try to convince him his actions matter, not his memory.

The entire film is a sleight of hand, the viewer never really knowing which part of his reality to grieve. Was Quaid changed by the Rekall experience, or was the Rekall experience changed by Quaid?

See also AJAR.

TRANSUBSTANTIATION refers to the phenomenon of altering the form of something into another form. Octopuses perform a sort of transubstantiation through autotomy, severing part of their own bodies to escape from danger. In a single instant, they flee, releasing their amputated tentacle into in the teeth of a moray eel, a shark. Some contort their bodies into the shapes of their enemies; they flush their skin with the same stripes and stippled markings of lionfish.

It seems miraculous how they change and morph into something different. But how exactly do they *allow* for the change that saves them? I think so often about the moment they break away and get free from their captors. I can't determine how choice factors into the process, whether their participation in the release requires active awareness and cooperation, or if it happens only at the purely instinctual level.

One day I tell a friend I am puzzled by how long this sorrow is taking me to come out from under, how I keep waiting for the release from it. "It doesn't work that way," she says. She touches my hand gently. "I'm so sorry to say that this isn't a thing you can think yourself out of, Kristin."

"I'm so sorry," she keeps repeating.

See also OCTOPUSES.

TWISTS are a kind of bend in a thing. In stories, they are unexpected turns of events.

I will keep imagining things not here—the way your hands folded, the Mystery Kristin Keane—possibilities the After Me is aware are not possible. Studying stories for so long pressed these strange possibilities into me. They are their own kind of manipulation of time, are they not?

In the final episode of *Quantum Leap*, the bartender asks Sam, "Can you accept what you see is reality?"

"Which reality do I accept?" Sam asks.

"Haven't you accepted both, looking in all those mirrors?"

Sam asks him if he's been controlling things. The bartender points to the mirror and says, "*He's* been leaping you through time."

The "he" the bartender gestures toward is Sam.

We learn that Sam's controlled righting the course of history through Project Quantum Leap the entire time, but Sam is never really sure—and neither is the audience—if the bartender is God or fate or time—or Sam himself. It's the viewer who gets to decide.

This is not an attempt to get over something I never will, but to understand it. I *am* trying to find a way for you and I to not part, and also navigate a certain kind of parting. Because of this, I shaped the future with this encyclopedia, in a way: I lined you up, the parts of the parts, searching for the story. While I waited for it to emerge, though, the plan to wrangle time became past tense—the same way *us* is now. Grief bifurcates everything; it has not only twisted my memory and my experience with time, but also has twisted the twisting.

Here I offer you another kind of ending: I go on as I said I do, but it is so very much still unfinished.

"Why do you do it?" I'd like to ask the Mystery Kristin Keane. "Why do you take other people's names?"

She'd bite her fingernails in thought. "People think it's about the money, but it's not."

"So what, it's just for the *rush* or something?"

"You know, when you're someone else, you're not the one holding the loss anymore," she'd say. "Like: I don't have to be that person who reaches but can no longer find her mother. There is no ordering, Kristin. This *is* the story."

She'd pick up her bag. She'd leave.

UNRAVEL. A few months before you disappeared, I dreamt of you waiting inside my ear with the sea. We had plans to attend a book fair, but I fled to wander the streets of downtown and suddenly a flap opened in the atmosphere like a corner of wallpaper peeling back. Then: I knew. I felt just how much you loved me, and I was lost in it—a whole day passed, and the sun began setting as I drifted inside that energy. When I tried phoning you, the only thing I could hear on the line was a message of you pleading for help. Though I ran to find you, it was already too late: every bit of sadness I had in worrying about the After Time had fastened itself to my feet.

B put his hand to my back and directed me to catch my breath when I woke up sweated, hyperventilating. That had never happened to me before—a kind of overwhelming panic which kept me awake in fear of slipping back underneath the wallpaper into the regret of the losses of my control: the moment in the elevator, the afternoon on the phone.

Though commonly meant as "tangle," an obsolete usage of "ravel" is *untangle*, a word containing a strange kind of duplicity.

Unravel, *tangle*. Ravel, *un*tangle.

See also KNOT.

VALVES control pressure and flow and are used in plumbing and systems that typically handle liquids. By definition, doors could be considered a type of valve. They can be opened, but can also be shut.

I used to listen at your door when you talked on the phone at night, describing your day. I listened at the door when you called another single mother of a boy who broke into our apartment. I listened at the door when you cried in the bathroom.

When my grandfather irrigated the persimmons, I stood at the end of the row in the trench watching the water slide toward me in a long channel from where he released the valve open. It flushed the ditch so that the rough parts floated to the top. I waited until the edge of my shoe caught the edge of the water, and then I'd jump over it.

Sometimes I worry you will find this all so grim and think I only swim in darkness. In 1907, writer Marcel Proust wrote to his friend and contemporary André Beaunier after his mother died: "Now there is one thing I can tell you: you will enjoy certain pleasures you would not fathom now. When you still had your mother, you often thought of the days when you would have her no longer. Now you will often think of days past when you had her. When you are used to this horrible thing that they will forever be cast into the past, then you will gently feel her revive, returning to take her place, her entire place, beside you." Proust tells Beaunier he will always be a kind of broken, but there is beauty in revealing more of his mother over time.

There is something I find so comforting about the promise of this message: someday this pain might turn off, and a new way of being with you will emerge, shifting this time which has felt endless into a compressed memory. It will become just a trench I jumped over before shutting its door.

"What I need is hope," you said so often.

All of this sadness, these dark corners: they are because I love you so. Right now, though, it is still so very hard for me to see anything else.

See also JUMP.

W is the twenty-third letter in the alphabet and can represent the third unknown variable in an equation, or the extra coordinate in the fourth dimensional space with x, y, and z.

The last time I talk to the collection agents, I plead with them. *I am Kristin Keane,* I say. *The real one.* I tell them I've lost my mother; I ask them to help me. I write to Loan-Confidant one last time, explaining the same. At a certain point, I stop answering the phone. Eventually, two letters arrive confirming the claims have been dropped, my name finally cleared of debts.

"What a relief," you'd say. You would have worried this whole time about the stress of it all, about me trying to solve the puzzle of the other Mystery Kristin Keane, I know.

Part of me vanished with you and a new part of me was made, like a wave. I suppose I have tried figuratively putting us there in some of these scientific and mathematical ideas: you as x, me as y. Those letters are so similar in shape, I have wondered about that border between them so often. Is the y only missing the line that makes x itself, or is it the other way around? Isn't an x just a y that crosses itself?

Maybe I am no longer y—but instead a w, the tail of my former self twisted back into a new kind of fold, one accounting for—or complicating—what time means to me now. W for what we are now together, made up mostly of myself, my imagination, and whatever space-time continuum absorbs my faith. Perhaps it is an end to us both, or a new beginning, or maybe it is just a new kind of math.

People like those kinds of stories, don't they? They're hopeful.

Time folds.

This is the different ending, the one we both didn't want: it is not tidy; there is no resolution. I told you I smile now, which is true, but it can't ever be the same. *I'm* not the same. We desire healing after death because we love the people left behind. I know because I want that for others. You would want that for me, too.

You have been missing for almost a year now. Has time done the work in closing part of me shut—or have I? It is true that writing you into me has done its own kind of work. This is not a healing because it can't be, but it *is* a way to pay attention.

Your friend wrote me, *I spoke to her before she went to the other side.* There it was again: this elusive other place. You wouldn't have wanted me to be bothered, so I set the letter aside for a few days like it was an object from your altar.

For now, you and I *are* at different borders—I am alive, and you aren't here. Maybe you are as you said you would be—everywhere, in every hummingbird and every grain of sand. Maybe you are not. Maybe you are here right now watching me trying to find a way to an ending.

Or maybe on the other side, another me lives with you in reverse: you are the daughter, and *I* am the mother—another Kristin Keane—and I raise you alone with your sister, and hold you in the air when you are a child and smile the way you smiled at me, and you are bad like I was bad sometimes. I bring you roses with their ends tied in wet paper towels. I give you everything I've got because my love is just as boundless. It is not perfect, this love I give you; no kind of love is. But it is forever, whatever that means.

Maybe on the other side I get sick, and you hold my hand in hospital rooms. Maybe on the other side, like me now, you are not a mother. And maybe there, on that side, when I tell you I love you, you say in return—as I used to say to you before you weren't here: *I love you more.*

Then maybe I hold your face in my hands—a different face than mine, but one I can see myself inside of, and I smile at your eyes and say, just as you did every time I said it to you: *My love, that is just not possible.*

WAITING FOR GODOT is a play by the Irish writer Samuel Beckett—the namesake of *Quantum Leap*'s protagonist. In the play, two characters wait on a country road for Godot, who never arrives. The setting never changes, and aspects of the play are circuitous—dialogue, imagery, even the appearance of a particular character. While political, ethical, and religious interpretations of this work exist, it is largely interpreted as existential, about suffering for things not there. Beckett also engages concepts of identity—the viewer/reader never knows if the characters are themselves or representations of others; one claims he is not the same character he arrived as in the previous act.

Some say the story of Alice was written as a critique of evolving mathematical theories during the 19th century, that the absurdity of Alice's circumstances in Wonderland were instantiations of non-Euclidian geometry. I'm not sure, but she waits in her circumstance as well, and in the end, Alice *does* get back, and Sam chooses not to.

J tells me she thinks about the fourth dimension, too, that she returns to Alice sometimes as we did when we were children.

I have to figure that out now, the new path forward. But I have B. I have J, and my father, and our family—all the friends who have given me so much grace.

There is light, and I will keep reaching.

See also AYRESHIRES.

WAVES are formed by energy moving through water generated by wind, tides, objects, seismic activity, and other things. Lizard tails regrow, spiders regenerate parts of their legs. When a sea cucumber is dismembered, each piece goes on, born again to life. Are these things like waves? Are they what they once were? Is a lizard's tail the same tail if a part of it—the stem from which it emerges—remains intact?

What about the sea? What about each new wave that crests over a break? What about how they roll to the sand?

I'm not sure I will ever be able to get Plutarch's paradox out from under me now.

Waves are also particles undulating in electromagnetic fields. They bend and reflect when they encounter obstacles in their paths.

They are also like emotions rising. Like sadness. Like grief.

You can wave with your hands. You can cup them in the air, curl your fingers around the atmosphere and move them back and forth.

You can say hello with this motion, and with your hands in the air the same way, suddenly change its meaning completely: a greeting can now become a goodbye.

WIGNER, EUGENE (1902-1995), a theoretical physicist, stated, "The present writer had occasion, some time ago, to call attention to the succession of layers of 'laws of nature,' each layer containing more general and more encompassing laws than the previous one and its discovery constituting a deeper penetration into the structure of the universe than the layers recognized before." Laws of nature, he goes on to argue, are not only unnatural, but so are their discoveries. Newton's law of gravity, which, when established, could only be reliably estimated at four percent accuracy, Wigner writes, was "repugnant to his time and to himself." Ptolemy's epicycles put Earth at the center of the universe, thinkers believing for centuries it was flat and hollow in the middle.

I will never give up hoping that someday we'll reflect on our views of the supposed limitations of another dimension in this same way—that a different math is possible. Ideas need both optimism and pathways for abandonment: we *could* be wrong. Wigner says theories considered proven could be upended by a bigger theory unavailable for discovery.

Perhaps one day a different dimension will emerge where we can be together, where you're just waiting to be discovered in the same way we found gravity, the same way we moved electrons. A wall dividing all the ones the rest of us have missed—who have held each other while waiting—will collapse. Then, we'll embrace, hold hands.

We will weep with relief.

See also DEVOTION.

X is an unknown variable; a thing we can't see: there, but also not. Something we try solving, and getting inside.

When I was twenty-four, you asked if I was all right. Do you remember that? Twenty-four held promise, but I was sinking. I couldn't tell you why. I couldn't even name it for myself. Do you remember all the times you asked? All the time, I said: *I'm fine, I'm fine, I'm fine.* Some days, when I'm missing you most, I imagine telling you what I felt like then. Sometimes, it's hard for me to even remember it.

I could not always break the water. I could not always surface over the wave caps of sorrow to pull you inside with me. The indecipherable "i" when you wrote my name for the last time: *I* am as shut as a vice. *I* am an atoll only *I* am allowed to swim inside of. *I* am seasick. *I* am sad. You asked me to let you in sometimes, and sometimes I couldn't.

"Are you okay?"

"Please, mother, stop with the questions," I said then.

You would laugh at that memory now—"Kristin, my love, is this encyclopedia not just completely full of *yours*?" you would ask. But, as always, you would pause, then offer grace by adding something like, "Now you understand questions are what you have when you are trying to understand a thing you love so much."

You told me at the end to lean, so: I'm trying.

Sometimes it feels good to be alone, you used to say. When I was a child, you'd close yourself in dark rooms with your migraines and I'd stand in the small shaft of light through the crack in the open door, and watch you put a washrag across your face. You did not want the sun or to look at anything but the dark. That's when I knew you were not yourself: you always loved the light.

An *x* is also something you make with your arms crossed at your collar bone to say: *Stop*. To say: *Leave me alone*. In *A Grief Observed*, C.S. Lewis writes that sorrow is not a condition you can illustrate exactly, but a kind of narrative one could potentially record forever. The griever has to make the choice to put an end to the accounting.

The Mystery Kristin Keane was never identified, but every time a call comes through I don't recognize, my stomach bends; it is something I see but also feel.

I do hope she is okay—whatever that means—wherever she is. *Whoever* she is.

See also Y.

Y is the twenty-fifth letter of the alphabet. It can act as a consonant or a vowel, the latter often pronounced as a long "i" as in "bye," "cry," "my." *Y* is not like the *question* why, though it sounds like the start of one.

I have been cataloging as a way to make sense of these things, of the empty space where you were. I thought if I taught you the way it feels—if I taught you about things you might no longer know—I too would understand better and find my way to a kind of ending. But the feeling of no longer having you here is not an emotion. It is not an animal or a person. It is not a song, or an instrument or something you can play. It is not something you can sing along with—or to. It is not violet, or crimson, or honey. It is not magenta—or the word "magenta." Nor is it silver or gold or chartreuse or a color—if you even know what that means anymore. It is not water or the Indian Ocean, or the Atlantic Ocean, or the Pacific Ocean. It is not a wave cap or the place you once stood in the sand. It is not the sand. It is not the shape your feet used to make in the sand, or the way the water washed those shapes away. It is not a seashell—or a bird, or a rose. It is not a peony. It is not a shaft of lavender. It is not any kind of flower. It is not condolence arrangements, or gravestones, or the cards given to mourners. It is not the act of mourning. It is not morning. It is not the sun rising. It is not the sun setting. It is not the stars and not the night and not the sky at night. It is not the moon or looking at the moon. It is not a word.

It cannot be named, but just lives inside of me even though you wouldn't want it to, even though you would want to relieve me of every part of it.

In the end, I didn't get what I wanted: more time with you. There was no invitation or desired ownership like *my* house, *my* job, *my* mother—the feeling I've inherited was just there the moment you disappeared, filling everything up with it. This is the part that will be hardest on your heart: in the end, that filling-everything-up-with-it feeling is what I got—something I believe entirely, would be unbearable for you to know I have. But it is here, and I have to keep going. I will probably never make sense of this, and maybe that is the point. Maybe that is what time does, how it shows us all its sides.

See also X.

ZEBRA FINCH are popular pet birds with zebra-like plumage at their necks, adjacent to rust-colored cheek patches and brightly colored beaks.

That finch I brought home in the shoebox, you put it in a cage. You fixed a small basket into the corner where it could sleep. You put a small scrap of fabric inside, the kind that comes with catalog samples. That finch was quiet in the cage for months as it hopped from one wooden dowel to the next.

At the pet store, you asked the man for another finch. You described the color of its beak, its plumes. He assured you the other finch was male, too, and would make for a platonic companion. But when those two finches met, they sang and sang. Then there were eggs, then more finches.

Once, they tossed a small chick with a newly formed beak into the bottom of the slats. You took it out with tenderness. You buried that baby in the yard. You said a prayer.

This is just one scene, chosen from all the scenes of you: the bird, the cage, the scrap of fabric, the pet store, the burial. That is what I miss most. The benevolence. Your careful heart.

I don't know what happened to those finches—I don't remember. That wouldn't be the first thing I'd ask you if I could. It wouldn't be the first thing I would say to you if I saw you again—but it would be something.

ZETA is most commonly understood as the sixth letter of the Greek alphabet, but an obsolete meaning of "zeta" is a kind of room, or chamber.

At a Vatican conference in 1981, Hawking proposed the universe perhaps arose from nothing at all. He said, "There ought to be something very special about the boundary conditions of the universe and what can be more special than the condition that there is no boundary?" From this, he postulated that the universe started from a point of zero, comprising the past, present and future all at once. It's a math I can't explain or understand, but the idea, I think, is beautiful.

The seasons change. I stop counting the days. Even the concept of the number of weeks since your disappearance has dissolved into a sort of amalgam. A freeze hits the city, and the leaves look like glass—or like the scorpions dipped in resin you brought me and J from Arizona—one on a keychain, the other in a small but hefty paperweight.

On a run through the park one day I approach the bridge, my turning point. The leaves shiver off the trees at the bridge's crest, so I stop for a moment to watch them. It is so cold outside, I am the only one running in the rain. When I stop, the water falls from the sleeves of my windbreaker as if they are long tongues waiting to recount a story.

I go to the spot where they come undone from their branches and wait. They are russet; their stems have shivered into a new color. Everything is shivering. I am shivering now that my body has stopped.

The leaves change. Not because they want to, but because they *have* to. Because time and the axis of the Earth force them to shift into something different—to literally turn a color unrecognizable to themselves. They don't choose that, just like they don't ask to unfasten from where they are anchored down: time does that, too.

Then they wilt. Shift shape. Soon, every small bit left of them will blow away, just like every speck of sand on the beach eventually will, too.

What can we hope? Kant asked. Maybe in another dimension we live inside my constructions of television sets—maybe we live in reruns, understanding they are fixed in time. There is something very beautiful about that idea to me now, too. The way I look at those things over and over again, conjuring you, like we are still in the same room together.

Maybe we end at the center of a black hole, us and everything else crushed by an infinite force. Maybe the force is gravity. Maybe it is our love.

INDEX of ENTRIES

Absolute Time

Afterlife

Ajar

Alice's Adventures in
   Wonderland

Alphabet

Altars

Arizona

Arrows

Ayrshires

Bakula, Scott

Barthes, Roland

Baseline

Beginning

Being

Between Time

Blaine, David

Blur

Border

Cabo San Lucas

Cast

Change

Channel

Childhood

Chronology

Crystals

Death

Devotion

Diagnosis

Einstein, Albert

Encyclopedias

Endings

Entry

Everything

Finch

Fix

Fog

Folds

Fourth Dimension

Fracture

Freud, Sigmund

Gestalt Empty Chair Technique

Ghosts

Goblets

Gone

Hawking, Steven

Home

Homesickness

Home Depot

Horology

Inertial Frame of Reference

Insomnia

Inspect

Jade

Jump

Kant, Immanuel

Kappa Effect

Knot

Kübler-Ross, Elizabeth

Labor

Leibniz, Gottfried Wilhem

Letters

Lungs

Magic

Many-Worlds Interpretation

Memories

Middle

Minkowski Spacetime

Mirage

Mirrors

Movies

Newton, Sir Isaac

Nonexistent Objects

Novikov Self-Consistency
    Principle

Octopuses

Other Side

Out of This World

Plutarch

Popeil, Ronald

Quantum Leap

Quantum Mechanics

Raft

Recognize

Residue

Returns

Sea

Singapore

Sorrow

Soul

Tarot

Taxidermy

Tides

Total Recall

Transubstantiation

Twists

Unravel

Valves

W

Waiting for Godot

Waves

Wigner, Eugene

X

Y

Zebra Finch

Zeta

WORKS REFERENCED

Allen, I. (Executive Producer). (1985-1985). *Alice in Wonderland* [TV series]. CBS.

Barthes, R. (1972). *Mythologies*. Farrar, Straus and Giroux.

Barthes, R. (1977). *Roland Barthes* (R. Howard, Trans.). Farrar, Strauss and Giroux.

Barthes, R. (1980). *New critical essays* (R. Howard, Trans.). Hill and Wang.

Barthes, R., Léger, N., & Howard, R. (2010). *Mourning diary: October 26, 1977-September 15, 1979*. Hill and Wang.

Beckett, S. (2006). *Waiting for Godot: A tragicomedy in two acts*. Faber and Faber.

Bellisario, D., Pratt, D., Zinberg, M., & Johnson, C. (Executive Producers). (1989-1993). *Quantum Leap* [TV series]. Belisarius Productions; Universal Television.

Berman, R., Roddenberry, G., Piller, M., Taylor, J., Hurley, M., & Wagner, M. (Executive Producers). (1987-1994). *Star Trek: The Next Generation* [TV series]. Paramount Television.

Blaine, D. (2012, June 14). *Swimming with Sharks*. [Video]. YouTube. https://youtu.be/cdglB8s-RaY

Bonanno, G. A. (2009). *The other side of sadness: What the new science of bereavement tells us about life after loss*. Basic Books.

Boni, J., Booker, B., Booker, B., Levine, L., & Yanok, G. (Executive Producers). (1987-1991). *Out of This World* [TV series]. Bob Booker Productions.

Burton, T. (Director). (1988). *Beetlejuice* [Film]. Warner Bros.

Carroll, L. (1866). *Alice's Adventures in Wonderland*. MacMillan and Co.

Carroll, L. (1871). *Through the looking-glass, and what Alice found there*. Macmillan and Co.

Cooper, B. (Director). (2018). *A Star Is Born* [Film]. Warner Bros.

David Blaine risks his life to break a world record. (2008, April 30). [TV series episode]. *The Oprah Winfrey Show*. Harpo Studios.

Diderot, D., & Alembert, J. L. R. (1751). *Encyclopédie: Ou Dictionnaire raisonné des sciences, des arts et des métiers*. Chez Briasson.

Franzblau, S. H. (2002). Deconstructing attachment theory: Naturalizing the politics of motherhood. In L. H. Collins, M. R. Dunlap, & J. C. Chrisler (Eds.), *Charting a new course for feminist psychology* (pp. 93–110). Praeger Publishers/ Greenwood Publishing Group.

Freud, S. (1913). *The Interpretation of Dreams* (A. A. Brill, Trans). MacMillan Co.

Freud, S., Strachey, J., & Gay, P. (1989). *The future of an illusion*. Norton.

Gord, K., Rosen, B., & Goodman, G. (Executive Producers). (1992-1998). *Highlander* [TV series]. David-Panzer Productions.

Hawking, S. (1982). *The boundary conditions of the universe*. In *Astrophysical Cosmology Proceedings* (pp. 563-572).

Hawking, S. (1989). *A brief history of time*. Bantam Books.

Hitchcock, A. (Director). (1960). *Psycho* [Film]. Paramount Pictures.

Hooper, T. (Director). (1982). *Poltergeist* [Film]. MGM; UA Entertainment Company.

Kant, I. (1899). *Critique of pure reason* (J. M. D. Meiklejohn, Trans.). Willey Book Co.

Kelly, C. (Director). (2016). *Other People* [Film]. Vertical Entertainment.

Kübler-Ross, E. (1969). *On death and dying*. Macmillan.

Kubrick, S. (Director). (1980). *The Shining* [Film]. Warner Bros.

Lambert, M. (Director). (1989). *Pet Sematary* [Film]. Paramount Pictures.

Leibniz, G. W., Remnant, P., & Bennett, J. F. (1896). *New essays on human understanding*. Macmillan.

Lewis, C. S. (1961). *A grief observed*. Seabury Press.

McCarthy, L., Nelson, G., Brush, B., Melvoin, J., Abrams, I., Harding, N., Dinner, M., LeVine, D., & Hargrove, D. (Executive Producers). (1996-2000). *Early Edition* [TV series]. Three Characters.

Netter, D., & Straczynski, J.M. (Executive Producers). (1993-1998). *Babylon 5* [TV series]. Warner Home Video.

Newton, I., Motte, A., & Chittenden, N.W. *Newton's Principia. The mathematical principles of natural philosophy*. New-York, D. Adee, 1848. Pdf. https://www.loc.gov/item/04014428/.

Nolan, C. (Director). (2014). *Interstellar* [Film]. Paramount Pictures.

Proyas, A. (Director). (1994). *The Crow* [Film]. Miramax.

Ronco. (1991). Electric Food Dehydrator [Advertisement].

Rovelli, C. (2018). *The order of time.* New York: Riverhead Books.

Scorsese, M. (Director). (1976). *Taxi Driver* [Film]. Columbia Pictures.

Serling, R. (Writer), Brahm, J. (Director). (1960, February 26). Mirror Image (Season 1, Episode 21) [TV series episode]. In B. Houghton (Producer), *The Twilight Zone.* Cayuga Productions.

Sutton, C. (1992). *Spaceship neutrino.* Cambridge University Press.

Verhoeven, P. (Director). (1990). *Total Recall* [Film]. TriStar Pictures.

Wigner, E. (1963, December 12). *Events, Laws of Nature, and Invariance Principles.* https://www.nobelprize.org/uploads/2018/06/wigner-lecture.pdf

Worden, J. W. (2008). *Grief counseling and grief therapy: A handbook for the mental health practitioner.* Springer Publishing Company.

Zucker, J. (Director). (1990). *Ghost* [Film]. Paramount Pictures.

ACKNOWLEDGEMENTS

I'm exceedingly grateful to those who helped bring this book to form by steeling my heart, ideas and words in myriad ways: Zed Adams, *Barrelhouse*, Lisa Brown, *Catapult*, John Baunach, Rebecca Childers, Lilly Dancyger, Carly Duncan, Katie Eller, Kathy Gibson, Steve Gibson, James Gregorio, Friends of the San Francisco Public Libraries, Daniel Handler, Jessica Henry, Mike Ingram, David Klein, Katrina McHugh, Nina Renata Aron, April Perroni, Thomas Ross, San Francisco Public Libraries, Stanford Libraries, John Stassen, Roxanne Taghavian, The Brown Handler Writer's Residency, The Ruby, Karoline Trepper, Ariana Wolf, Holly Woods. Grateful/ lucky for and indebted forever to: Athena Costis, Connie Dalton, Loretta Dalton, Ron Dalton, Richard Keane for their devotion, support, care, and showing me just exactly how to make endings beautiful; to my sister, J—for Alice, for jam, for encouragement, for our love; and, to B—for our life together, for how it keeps blooming, for everything. There will never be enough time.

ABOUT the AUTHOR

Kristin Keane is the author of the novella *Luminaries* (Omnidawn, 2021). Her work has appeared in *The Normal School*, *The New England Review*, *Electric Literature* and elsewhere. She is a doctoral fellow at Stanford University where she researches the teaching and learning of literacy.

Effortless, genuine, and balanced.
My forever vow.